GETTING
PREPARED
by Robin Egerton

with Angela England

—— AN ——

untrained HOUSEWIFE
GUIDE

Printed in the United States of America
First Printing, 2013

ISBN-13: 978-0-615-77708-5

Angela England Media
4019 W. Hwy 70 #252
Durant, OK 74701

www.angelaenglandmedia.com

Ordering Information:
Quantity sales. Special discounts are available on quantity purchases by corporations, associations, and others. For details, contact the publisher at the address above.

Printed in the United States of America

FOREWORD

Being prepared for an emergency is a prudent thing. Each day, the news is filled with accounts of floods, tornadoes, earthquakes, hurricanes, and other natural disasters. How many of the people involved were actually ready to face the aftermath of these disasters? How many became dependent on others for their every need?

Since I first started selling long-term storage food in 1994, none of these disasters have gotten any easier to survive nor predict. To top it off, our economy has taken a nose dive during this time, and no one knows from one day to the next whether they will have a job. Being prepared to take care of your family when you are out of a job for a few weeks or months brings an enormous amount of peace of mind.

Natural disasters are not all that we need to be concerned with in the era we are living in. Continued increase in taxation has brought many families' income down to the poverty level. Getting creative to make ends meet is really a form of preparing for hard times. As our economy continues to spiral downward, each family needs to have a plan of what they will do to deal with less money in the bank and higher prices in the store. Learning to garden and preserve your own food will not only save money at the grocery store, but most likely at the doctor's office. When you eat fresh foods and foods prepared without preservatives, artificial colors, and artificial sweeteners, your body is healthier. Many slight changes can be made today to make the coming economic hard times a bit easier.

"Store what you use and use what you store" is really not just a cliché, it is a way of life. This applies far beyond the reaches of food storage items. Knowing how to start a fire when it's raining and knowing how to build a shelter without power tools are things a family can practice and have fun doing, all while preparing themselves in case they find themselves braving the elements after a storm hits their area. Using a clothesline to dry your clothes will save money and prolong the life of your clothes. Turning first to your herbal first aid kits saves a trip to the doctor and gets you familiar with the items you are storing.

Knowing where to start preparing and knowing what to do with the items you buy is vital. Many people stock up on a grain mill to grind the pails of wheat they buy, but they have no idea how to bake a loaf of bread or prepare any food items that don't come from a mix. Learning now makes life during a disaster so much easier to handle.

Never take what you have for granted and never feel that you are in a "safe zone." Tornadoes can strike suddenly where they never have before. Rivers can reach their "100 year" flood levels in an overnight storm and secure jobs can be lost in an instant. No one is safe from any sudden disaster or long-term reaches of a failing economy.

"And said, Naked came I out of my mother's womb, and naked shall I return thither: the LORD gave, and the LORD hath taken away; blessed be the name of the LORD." Job 1:21

Jodi Hein
Owner, Homestyle Mercantile
www.HomestyleMercantile.com

Acknowledgements

Robin - Becoming a published author has been on my bucket list for quite some time. I will be forever grateful to Angela England for providing the opportunity for me to do so. I am not fully aware of all the hard work that goes into publishing a book, digital or otherwise, but there is no doubt that Brannan Sirratt — and probably some others - put in many hours making this book come to pass. Much thanks to them all!

Angela - This first step into self-published guides in the Untrained Housewife brand is the first of many amazing things to come, and I'm so grateful for those who have supported this vision along the way. Thank you to Robin for your knowledge contributed to this book — you are the perfect person to share your prepping knowledge. Thank you to Brannan and Becky for making it come together so beautifully. This is a book to be proud of!

TABLE OF CONTENTS

Foreword..iii

Acknowledgements v

SECTION I: PREPARING TO PREPARE

Chapter One - Getting Started
Beginning Preparedness..14

Must-Have Items..16

Chapter Two - First Priorities
Insurance..19

Food Storage 21

Water Storage..22

Generators for Heat and Electricity.............................23

72-Hour Survival Kits..25

The Ideal 72-Hour Emergency Kit...............................25

SECTION II: PREPARING AROUND THE HOUSE

Chapter Three - Kitchen Supplies
Keep the Kitchen Convenient.......................................31

Canning Equipment...34

Chapter Four - Canning Food for Storage
Pressure Canning 37

Processing Times And Pressures For Pressure Canners..............40

Bulk Canning for Emergency Preparedness.................42

Chapter Five - Storing Dry Foods
Storing and Managing Protein Sources.........................48

How to Store Grains..50

Long-Term Storage of Sweeteners................................54

Chapter Six - Shoes and Clothing for Emergencies
Some Things to Consider...57

Planning for Winter 60

Clothing for Summer...61

Selecting Good Shoes 62

Chapter Seven - Emergency Sources of Heat and Light
An Efficient Lighting Source: Kerosene Lamps.............64

A Practical Heating Source: Firewood 66

Tools Needed for Gathering Firewood..........................67

Safety Concerns Regarding Firewood 68

Homemade Fire Starters..70

Chapter Eight - Sanitation

Making Pottying as Pleasant as Possible 72
Homemade Wet Wipes...73
When You Don't Want to Potty Outside 74
Diapers During a Long-Term Crisis..................................75
Determine Your Diapering Needs 76
Washing Cloth Diapers 79
Feminine Hygiene in Disaster Scenarios 81

Chapter Nine - Buying Supplies

What to Look For at Yard Sales 87
In Fantasyland: Top of the Line Resources 90

SECTION III: PREPARING FOR ACTION

Chapter Ten - Menu Planning for a Month

Taking a Food Shortage One Month at a Time.................96
Building a 30 Day Emergency Menu Plan 99
Turning Recipes into a Meal Plan................................... 102
Breakfast Menu – One Month.. 105
Dinner Menu – One Month 105

Chapter Eleven - Foraging: Eating From the Yard

Edible Weeds.. 106
Edible Landscaping.. 109

Chapter Twelve - Laundry in Emergencies

Laundry Soap and Supplies... 113
Homemade Laundry Soap 113
Washing Laundry Outside 115
Drying Clothes Without Power.. 115

Chapter Thirteen - Battling the Elements

Hot Weather Safety 119
Heat Exhaustion 120
Heat Stroke.. 121
Cold Weather Safety 122
Frostbite... 123
Hypothermia.. 124
Shelter in Extreme Temperatures.................................... 126

Chapter Fourteen - Health and Safety

Specific Health Conditions 127
Diabetes, High Blood Pressure, Heart Conditions 128
Mental Health 129
Gastric and Internal Disorders....................................... 129
Breaks, Sprains, Strains... 129
Pregnancy.. 130
Physical Skills to Learn and Practice 130

Chapter Fifteen - Major First Aid
Basic First Aid Kits.. 131
Herbal First Aid... 132
Major First Aid 135
Unexpected Home Births.. 137

Chapter Sixteen - Natural Disasters
Establish Your Safe Place.. 140
What You Need in Your Safe Place 141
Immediate Needs After the Storm..................................... 142
A Reminder About Insurance 142
Pets and Emergency Situations 144
Have an Emergency Kit Prepared and Ready.......................... 144
Plan for Housing 145
Never Evacuate Your Home Without Your Pet 146
Make Sure All Family Members Are Aware of Your Disaster Plan. 146

Chapter Seventeen - Learning Together About Survival Situations
Fun Family Preparedness Activities.................................... 148
Fires.. 152
Tornadoes.. 153
Power Outages 154
Learn and Grow With Your Community.............................. 155

APPENDIX A
Essential Items for Emergency Situations........................... 160

APPENDIX B
Yard Sale Check List Organizer.. 164

APPENDIX C
Essential Items for a Home First Aid Kit 166

APPENDIX D
Resources... 168

SECTION I
PREPARING TO PREPARE

"Despair is most often the offspring of ill-preparedness"

Don Williams, Jr.

CHAPTER ONE
GETTING STARTED

Often, when we ask people if they are prepared for an emergency, they do not understand the question. They imagine the terms "Doomsdayer," "Survivalist," or "Prepper" — some crazy nut planning for world collapse. In fact, nothing could be further from the truth. When we change the question to, "How do you get through a power outage," we often hear simply that they have a generator. Ask if they have fuel for that generator, and the answer is usually limited to a sheepish grin.

An emergency can be a widespread, national or even world crisis. Usually, however, emergencies are very small and local — often they affect only your own family. This book is a guide to preparing your family for one month of any disaster that you can imagine, reasonably. We suggest ways you can prepare for a major power outage resulting from a blizzard, an earthquake or an ice storm. We suggest ways to have light, heat, and sanitation if there is no electricity. We suggest ways to prepare the family emotionally as well as physically for what otherwise could be a stressful time.

To answer the question of why to prepare, or what the goal of this book might be -- it is ultimately self-reliance. Our strategy is to have the capacity to be completely self-reliant for 30 days. Some will ask why so little, and others will ask why so much. We feel that if we can handle being completely on our own for one month, then a three-day power outage will be almost fun! If you feel your family needs to prepare for a longer period of time, 30 days is an excellent foundation to work from.

Why is this so important to us? Peace of mind! Emergency preparedness is important to us simply because we want to know that our families will be as comfortable, safe and healthy as they can reasonably be in any situation. That provides peace of mind to us, and we want to share that with you.

Beginning Preparedness

It is scary to consider how life could be. We are so spoiled as citizens of America at this particular time in history. But history does repeat itself, and with current events as they are, we should probably prepare ourselves for a bumpy ride. If nothing dramatic ever happens, we will at least have gained a positive experience and had some fun life lessons with our kids as we prepared. Let me repeat: *There is nothing to be lost from preparing your family for the worst, even if the worst never happens.*

Nobody likes hard times, but the key to getting through them - besides the obvious being prayer - is preparedness! And, if you are planning ahead anyway, why not plan for as many comforts as you can?

A generator can make power outages more comfortable even if you have not yet made many other preparations.
(Photo Credit to JMR_Photography on Flickr)

Consider where you live. Are you in tornado alley? Are you in a hurricane zone? On an earthquake fault? Do you live in a rural or urban area? Or, do you simply want to prepare to be able to stop buying groceries for one month when the car needs a repair? Plan your emergency preparedness based on your own situation.

A note from Robin: I live out in the country on wooded acreage. So, we are able to cut firewood and dump out potty buckets. The city-dwellers that lived through Hurricane Sandy on the U.S. East Coast have a different perspective, no doubt. I cannot figure out how I would handle personal hygiene and human waste if I lived in a big city apartment complex, but you might not be able to imagine living in a rural area.

You may want to prepare to live self-sufficiently all the time — which requires tools, etc. — or it might be better for your family to simply purchase what you need for just one month, such as already-cut firewood and a kerosene heater (with the kerosene!), rather than fussing with chainsaws.

Only you can know what your family needs, so consider your own situation, and plan accordingly.

Must-Have Items

- *Food and Water* are extremely important, obviously. This includes not only the food and water themselves, but the supplies and means to prepare them, if needed. That includes, but is not limited to, fuel, firewood, and proper cookware. Don't forget a method to purify the water.
- *Emergency Kits* - This Must-Have includes, but is not limited to, survival items for 72-hours, a carry bag, and first aid supplies.
- *Communication* - This can be a Must-Have if you are stranded, perhaps in the rubble from an earthquake or tornado, or if a simple power outage makes conventional phones inoperable. Consider a battery powered or solar powered two-way radio. Don't forget the batteries!
- *First Aid* - Antiseptic, antibacterial and perhaps antibiotic resources are all necessary. A suture kit and bandages for the possibility of a major wound are also Must-Haves.
- *Heat* - Absolute Must-Haves include blankets, extra sets of warm clothing, and a heat source with the requisite fuel. You can never have too many dry socks.
- *Light* - Candles, matches, kerosene lanterns, or flashlights are all important to have. Once more, don't forget the batteries!
- *Sanitation* - Must-Haves for sanitation that should be considered are feminine hygiene products, diapers, cloths, and a comfortable place to "go."
- *Tools* - Must-Have tools especially include those that do not re-

quire fuel. Additionally, you can never have too much WD-40, duct tape, ropes, tarps, etc.

- *Fuel* - Fuel is certainly a Must-Have if your other items require it! Sort of like batteries, some things are useless without stocking their vital components.
- *Don't forget your pets* - Pet food and other supplies are also Must-Haves for the animals in your family.

With these in mind, you can create a basic list of items to start gathering over time. We have also compiled our own, more specific list of important items to collect, and it can be found in *Appendix A – Essential Items for Emergency Situations*. Your needs may differ, but these lists should provide you with a good working foundation to get things going. Make a copy, or use them as a jumping-off point to make your own so that you have something to follow as you begin preparing your home and family for emergencies.

CHAPTER TWO
FIRST PRIORITIES

In the event of a major national disaster, the chances are good that the power grid will go down and we will not have access to our usual supplies and sources of energy. Think about the power going out right at this moment. Do you have food on hand that does not need to be cooked? Do you have drinkable water? In the short term, you'll be fine with just those two things. After a few days, though, you will want some good food, and you will want to freshen up a bit. What then?

So much can be wrapped up in a power outage. It may just be a transformer blown from a lightning storm – but it could be a major disaster that brings damage to the area, even your home, and takes time to repair. You should have adequate insurance to cover repairs, as we will discuss in a moment, but do you know what your plan covers? Do you know who to contact and what steps to take, even if the papers are inaccessible due to the circumstances? In the wake of Hurricane Sandy, one survivor spoke of his struggle to contact his insurance after his home flooded. Even though he was prepared with flood insurance, the papers were washed away, and the phone number he had available did not reach the agent.

Especially with weather-related disasters, turmoil in the atmosphere often means that one event is not the end. We often see storms causing major devastation, only to be followed by a cold snap or more storms immediately after. Many parts of the country are prone to extreme temperatures for a good portion of the year, with cold weather causing the most concern. Having a plan to heat your home in times of disaster is a very basic way to keep your family safe and warm should anything happen.

If all of this sounds terribly overwhelming, a good place to begin is with the immediate. Start by preparing for 72 hours, and then build further stores around that. Any preparation is better than none, and to be really prepared, we have to think of as many scenarios as possible and form a plan – then, hopefully, we will never have to put those plans in place.

Insurance

Homeowner's insurance is not very expensive, and it is common to roll the monthly premium into your mortgage payment along with taxes in a fund called escrow. Homeowner's insurance can be as little as $100/month, rolled into your payment, so you don't even know it's there. It can provide you a tremendous amount of peace of mind during a disaster.

Keep your paperwork in a safe and accessible spot, with copies stored outside of your home, such as in a bank safe deposit box. Keep copies of contact information for your insurance company elsewhere, as well. Learn the details of your insurance coverage so that you can formulate a plan for when disaster strikes.

KNOW WHERE TO GO RIGHT AFTER THE STORM. Homeowner's insurance can provide you an instant voucher to stay in a hotel immediately after the crisis. It can also provide food, immediate replacements of necessities such as clothing and toiletries, and perhaps even temporary transportation to work. Some plans also provide a place to rent while you are in the process of rebuilding or searching for a new house, and some will pay your rent for a certain period of time.

KNOW HOW TO REBUILD. Homeowner's insurance is designed to pay off your existing mortgage and then help you take out another one, either to rebuild your old home or to purchase a new house. You will still have a mortgage, but it will be on your new or rebuilt home.

KNOW WHAT TO DO ABOUT YOUR STUFF. Homeowner's insurance can also provide extra money to replace the contents of your home. Total replacement is the best option, in which you will receive the cost to replace your appliances, furniture, etc., rather than just the current value. This can matter a great deal if you have old or used contents.

Take photographs of every room in your house so that you have a record of what you need to have replaced. Open cupboards and take pictures. This is not to document your level of tidiness, but rather to prompt your memory. When you see the outer items of a cupboard, you will be more likely to remember what is in the back. Put the photos in a safe place, away from the home, along with a list of contents that would need to be replaced. Do not forget to include appliances, electronics, and heirlooms, as well as identifying information such as serial numbers, if possible.

A home safe might be a good option if it is strong enough to withstand the high winds of a tornado and the high heat of a wild fire. Another terrific option is a bank safety deposit box. They only cost around $20 *per year!* This is very affordable for the peace of mind it offers. A free option is a friend or relative's home in a region quite far away from where you live. You don't want to keep it near your home, because a natural disaster could damage both areas. If you store your photographs on a digital device, be sure it is up to date. For example, if you currently have important information on a floppy disk, it will be very difficult, if not impossible, to retrieve that information.

WHAT IF YOU RENT? Homeowner's insurance is not just for homeowners. There are renter's policies, as well, that will cover the contents of your rented home or apartment. While you are at it, check on your liability level should a fire start in your apartment, perhaps from a candle or defective electrical item.

KNOW WHAT KIND OF INSURANCE TO BUY. Shop for homeowner's insurance like you shop for anything else. Consider the biggest risks in your area, and check on the availability of earthquake, tornado, flood and fire insurance. Find out about insurance coverage if someone drives a car into your house. Check on insurance coverage if somebody gets hurt at your house. Ask about discounts and package prices; often, discounts are available if you buy both your auto and home insurance from the same provider.

As difficult as it would be to lose your home and the contents therein, imagine the huge relief of automatically having a place to live, money to replace the immediate necessities, and money to replace your stuff. That peace of mind is absolutely worth the minimal monthly costs of quality homeowner's insurance.

Food Storage

To begin food storage, start with what you already use, and then build from there. If you build your home store around your menu and your menu around your home store, you will not have to adjust your palates to a new diet when the time comes to use it. Wouldn't it be a huge comfort, as well as convenient, if during a major national disaster, your family's eating habits could remain the same? What a great morale booster that would be!

A note from Robin: As an independent consultant for Shelf Reliance, I am a bit biased towards many, but not all, of their long-term "Thrive" food products. Fresh fruits, veggies, meat and dairy for storage are all items I recommend purchasing from a supplier you can trust, which for me is Shelf Reliance. Other basics may be found elsewhere for much, much less money — I am thinking of wheat, beans, rice, etc. However, consider that those items must be cooked in some way and prepare accordingly.

Water Storage

Obviously, we cannot live without water, and if it is not free of harmful bacteria, we cannot live with it, either. Unfortunately, water is very difficult to store in large quantities for a long term disaster. Still, there are ways to handle this.

Water can be stored in empty bleach bottles that you do not rinse out first. It could be drinkable if necessary and is certainly good for washing. Water can also be stored in glass jars that have been pressure canned for long-term storage. That is quality drinking water, but again, it is impossible to store enough for an entire family for months.

For long-term water storage, a water purification system of some sort is absolutely essential. There are many ways to accomplish this: small kits to purify individual servings, filtration pumps, purification tablets and 55-gallon supply kits. Again, this is going to come down to what works for your family and level of preparation.

When considering a water supply without electricity,

- We do not need to bathe/shower as much as we do now. All that really needs to be washed daily are the "stinky parts." Give each member of the family their own color for washcloths and it will be easy to keep everything as hygienic as possible.
- We do not need to launder our clothing as much as we do. If we are in a survival situation, we should probably just prepare ourselves to be dirtier than usual. (We know, *yuck!*)

- We generally waste an enormous amount of water in our daily activities. A fun family project would be to catch all water that is normally wasted and place it in a barrel. See how long it takes the family to fill it up. Think about running water while brushing your teeth, emptying out ice from glasses after meals, and running individual baths. Learning to conserve water will help a lot in a survival situation; your morale will be stronger if you are already used to conserving water.

A note from Angela: When we had the big drought in summer of 2011 and our city was faced with a watering ban, we were able to keep the garden productive by using gray water from our bathtub and dishwashing water. You never know what your emergency may be, but for us, keeping our garden growing in triple-digit weather took some creative water management.

- Consider how you will water your pets and livestock. You should know how to get your hands on enough water for your pet for a few days. A week is a good minimum to have access to at all times.
- Consider how much pure water you will need if you have a baby on infant formula. It's hard to store enough gallons of fresh water for a prolonged emergency situation, so that's a time where a water filtration system would come in handy.
- Consider how you will manage diapers. One option is to simply buy a 30-day supply of diapers. If the situation lasts longer than one month, however, then what? It is a good idea to have a supply of cloth diapers on hand at all times. As with clothing, there will likely be a need to wash cloth diapers during an emergency. See tips for washing laundry indoors or out with a limited water supply in *Chapter 12 – Laundry in Emergencies.*

Generators for Heat and Electricity

The most important part of preparing for the future might be to study the past. Survival Spot has put together a list of the "Top 100

Items to Disappear First During a National Emergency" (For your own reference, print off our take on the top items to stock up on in *Appendix A* at the end of the book.) The top five items include a power source (generator), water and sanitation, and lighting and heat. Securing these items now will put you several steps ahead of the curve in an emergency situation down the road.

We have a gas generator at our house. They are easily obtained at a variety of stores and run from $300-$800 at Sears. However, we are really bad about storing gasoline for it. Dumb, huh? Gasoline is very difficult to store, so the likelihood of being able to depend on a generator for any length of time is not very good. When we have twenty gallons or so on hand, we can use the generator a few times a day to flush toilets, take hot baths and keep the refrigerator and freezer cold. Our house is wired so that we can plug the generator into a main box on the outside of the house and run certain circuits from it – toilets, freezer/refrigerator and stove. This is a great comfort and convenience in the short term, but not for a lengthy national disaster.

A propane generator is a better choice. Propane is more easily stored – think of the big silver propane tanks. One could be purchased and filled, and then you would be able to run a generator for a long time. Remember, preparation and foresight equals long-term comfort and convenience.

> *Tip: It is possible to convert a gasoline generator to propane for less than $300!*

Battery and solar powered generators are also an option. These can be stored a head of time, or you can use solar panels to recharge them. This would be the best option for a long term disaster and can run from $130-$1500.

Do you NEED a generator in an emergency? Consider the following:
- How long are you preparing for? Days? Weeks? Months? Years? Short-term power outages can be managed fairly easily without a generator, if not comfortably and conveniently. A full freezer will

stay frozen for several days. By using a pressure canner more than the freezer, you can extend your lack of dependence on electricity by weeks or even months.

- Does anyone in your house have a life-sustaining need for power? Oxygen? Kidney dialysis? Heart monitor? C-Pap machine? A generator would be prudent under these circumstances.
- Do you have access to wood? Firewood provides heat for shelter, cooking and purifying water. We live around the woods, so we are designing our preparedness plan to depend more on wood than electricity. We already have a fireplace insert to provide heat and a place to do some light cooking or reheating. Wood can also be used for outside cooking and dutch-oven cooking.

We all want to be comfortable for as long as possible in any given situation, and a generator provides that in the short-term. For the long-term, prepare for the worst and hope for the best!

72-Hour Survival Kits

In major disasters where the entire area is devastated — such as Hurricane Katrina, Hurricane Sandy, or the tornadoes in Joplin, MO — it takes time for emergency crews to gain access. Whether it is FEMA, the Red Cross, the electric company or even church volunteers, they cannot help you until after the storm passes. Then there are often infrastructure issues — roads may be impassable, and FEMA trucks that are waiting just outside the scope of the storm may be a day away. Needs have to be assessed. Insurance adjusters are overwhelmed. All of this takes time — at least three days. So, it is important that you can take care of yourself until help can get to you.

The Ideal 72-Hour Emergency Kit

FOOD - MREs (Meals Ready to Eat) are the most efficient source of food for a three day period. They are small, lightweight, and do not require cooking or heating. Protein bars are a good addition, as well as a bit of candy. Select hard candy, as other types might melt in storage.

WATER - It is difficult to store three days of drinkable water for an entire family. The most efficient alternative is water purification tablets. They are small, light-weight, and you can use them with whatever water you may find available. Camping Survival offers a survival straw that would be ideal for an emergency kit; the water is purified as it is sipped through the straw.

When planning for surviving for 72 hours, forget about washing. You can get by with being a bit smelly for 3 days, and it is not practical to store washing water.

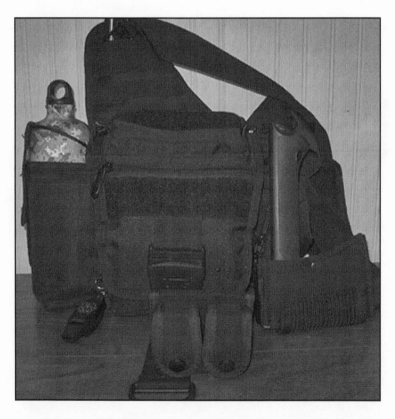

Your 72-hour bag should not be large, so plan appropriately sized items as you pack it. (Photo Credit to TheMKShop on Flickr)

PERSONAL HYGIENE - Include in your 72-Hour Emergency Kit sanitary napkins and/or tampons, "wet wipes," and diapers if necessary. If you have the room in your kit, you can include deodorant and other niceties, but remember, the goal for this particular kit is surviving for three days until help arrives.

SHELTER - Depending on your location and situation, you may want to include a tent in your kit. Certainly include some heat-retaining blankets that are lightweight. These can be found in any camping section of any retail store. After storms, we often find ourselves wet, and that makes for chilly nights, even in warm climates.

RECREATION - A deck of playing cards or UNO cards are lightweight and will help pass the time. Patience is not something you can include in your pack, but it is essential that you have it!

When planning your 72-hour kit, start with just that – enough to endure the first 72 hours of anything. Be sure your kit is portable so that you can take it with you should your home and other supplies be destroyed. If you have a safe place, like a tornado shelter, keep your kits there. Do not make them too elaborate; this is bare minimum thinking.

After you have your family's 72-hour survival pack ready, expand on it. Once you can make it for 72 hours, start preparing for a week. Then two weeks. Then one month! If you feel you need to be prepared for a longer period of time, just keep on doing what you are doing and your efforts will pay off in the end.

SECTION II
PREPARING AROUND THE HOUSE

"An idea can only become a reality once it is broken down into organized, actionable elements."

Scott Belsky

CHAPTER THREE
KITCHEN SUPPLIES

We may not realize it in our modern age, but life really does center around the kitchen. Something else we may not realize is how electrical our kitchen is. We use electric stoves, refrigerators, blenders, mixers, juicers and even can openers! During a storm, or when the power goes out, we can find our lives literally stalled when we cannot heat, cool, grind, mix or even open our food. One way to prepare your family for a power outage is to take note of what equipment you routinely use, and then figure out how to complete the same job without electricity. If you change your lifestyle accordingly by juicing, mixing and opening by hand, you will not even notice when the power is out.

Keep the Kitchen Convenient

If we are forced to live without electricity for several days or weeks, what kitchen utensils would we want the most?

CAN OPENER - Do you have an electric can opener? That's great! But do you have a manual can opener Just-In-Case? With a manual can opener, you can open any canned food and eat it straight out of the can without heat. So, in this scenario, which is more important – a heating source for cooking or a can opener? A manual can opener wins, hands down!

MIXERS - How many meals can you prepare without mixing some-thing up? Do you have an electric mixer? A Bosch and a hand mixer are both great to have in a day to day kitchen, but what if the power is out for any length of time? Homestyle Mercantile has an adapter to turn their electric mixer in to a hand crank mixer, or a plain, old hand whisk will replace your hand mixer in most cases. You can never go wrong having a supply of wooden spoons in a drawer somewhere.

Possibly the most important kitchen tool you can have is a can opener. What use are canned goods if you cannot open them?
(Photo Credit to Vasenka on Flickr)

GRINDERS AND BLENDERS - Are you ready to make your own flour if necessary? Having 40 pounds of wheat and a hand grinder is practical, common sense. Even if you don't want to make your own breads on a regular basis, I recommend both learning how and stocking up on the supplies and equipment as part of getting prepared.

A note from Robin: What do you use your electric blender for? Everything I use mine for — and I don't use it often — my family can easily do without during a major power outage. So, I personally have no alternative plans for my blender. What about you?

ELECTRIC GRIDDLES, ROASTERS, AND CROCK POT - Everyone who will read this likely relies on at least one of these, if not all three! Plan out a month's worth of menus that will consolidate your cooking method to using just one. (Don't forget to have all of the ingredients stocked up.) For instance, plan a month's worth of meals that can be cooked in one pot: soups, stews, grain cereals, etc. Try this until you find your preferred method, then have the necessary pot and a way to use it on hand.

Perhaps you would want a tripod that hangs over a wood fire and to prepare to cook all meals outside. Perhaps, you would like a course in dutch-oven cooking. A camp stove is a good idea, but be sure you have a month's supply of fuel. The camping section of most stores will carry griddles to be used on a camp stove or on an open fire.

Survival Spot suggests that charcoal and lighter fluid will be some of the items that are hard to find in an emergency. If you do not have access to wood, then stockpiling a supply of charcoal (and lighters!) will be a necessity if you want any hot foods.

DUTCH OVEN COOKING UNITS - Dutch oven cooking is a convenient way to bake outdoors – from main dishes to desserts and breads. One way to cook with a Dutch oven is to heat charcoal briquettes on your open fire. Once they are lit, pull them away from the main fire, but still within the fire pit. Set the Dutch oven on top of the number of briquettes called for in your recipe, place the lid on, and then set the required number of briquettes on top of the lid.

Another way to use a Dutch oven outdoors is to dig a pit slight larger than the oven itself. Byron Bills from Byron's Dutch Oven Cooking Page suggests the following:

"Line the sides of the hole with flat stones and check to make sure the oven will fit in the hole. Next, start a campfire in the bottom of the hole to get coals going. Keep adding wood to the fire until the hole is ½- ⅔ full of coals. Next, kick the fire out and remove the larger pieces of remaining wood. Dig a hole in the coals that the Dutch oven containing the evening meal can be set in, then cover the Dutch oven with the remaining coals (you want at least 2-3" of coals on top of the lid) followed by a 2" layer of dirt spread out over the coals. Spread 2 wet burlap bags over the dirt and cover them with rocks so they won't be blown away in the event a wind comes up. The burlap bags will help to hold the heat in. Then leave the oven to sit for the day. When you return to camp in the evening the food will be ready for eating. Simply dig the oven up and brush it off with a whisk broom prior to opening it."

Your Dutch oven requires some special care, but if you purchase a new one, it will come with directions such as seasoning it, not cooking acidic foods in it, not using soap when washing it, and allowing it to air dry.

Canning Equipment

A great portion of our emergency food preparedness plan relies on a pressure canner. We preserve everything! Of course, if you eat what you can *(maybe because you hate to cook, like me! – Robin)*, you need to keep canning on a regular basis and not just once for your pantry. Canned goods are convenient to simply open and heat, but the store-bought cans are expensive and full of unhealthy preservatives. So, if you can make your own convenience food, it will be cheaper and healthier, with the benefit of also coming in handy should you be without power for any length of time.

PRESSURE CANNERS - We absolutely, without a doubt, recommend the All American Canner. If you have or anticipate having a very large family, get the really big one – it holds 2 layers of 7 quart jars! The regular size holds 7 quart jars, or stacks of 15 pint jars. It uses a metal-to-metal seal, so there is no rubber gasket to go bad or cause explosive accidents. The canner is expensive, but it is a one-time purchase.

CANNING JARS - Canning jars do not have to be purchased new. They are usually available at yard sales and auctions, or better yet, just ask your elderly neighbor if they have any in their attic or basement. They likely do!

If given the choice, wide mouthed jars are simply easier to get stuff out of, but there is absolutely nothing wrong with small mouth jars. It is certainly not worth passing up a good deal on a small mouthed jar in order to pay full price for wide ones. Do check for nicks or chips on the edge of the jar before you buy it.

You will want quart jars for things like main entrees, vegetables and fruits. Pint jars are good for jams and jellies, smaller lunch portions of an entrée, and ground meat. A pint jar holds approximately one pound of ground meat. You will want half-pint jars for jams and jellies, gifts, ground meat, and candles. A half-pint jar of ground meat is perfect for one pizza!

RINGS AND LIDS - Rings will be used over and over. Again, we have never bought any new. Look at yard sales, auctions, and grandma's basement. Lids can only be used one time — unless you invest in reusable lids, which is on our list of things to do when we get extra money *(Ha!)*.

> *Tip: You do NOT have to cook meat before you can it.*

STORAGE SPACE - Think ahead about where to put your jars after canning. The optimal storage environment is in a conditioned air space – inside the house, or in a cool spot like a basement or cellar. A hot garage or storage shed or an attic will work, but it will significantly shorten the shelf life.

Build or buy shelves, or get creative by stacking cases into an end table. Stack two cases of filled quart jars and cover with a table cloth. Place cases of canned food under beds or in cupboards that are not currently being used for anything else. Be creative. You will be glad you went to the effort if you encounter a week-long power outage.

Getting the kitchen ready for a major calamity can seem overwhelming because so much of the rest of the preparedness plans hinges on keeping everyone fed and warm. Don't let yourself be fooled into ignoring preparation because it seems too big, though. Break it down into manageable steps. Sell your electric kitchen tools and use the money to buy hand tools. This will also free up the space you used to reserve for the larger appliances, allowing room to store more.

Plan on continuing your current menu plans and favorite meals during a disaster, and learn to do them with minimal or no electricity. Learn to can your own convenience foods, saving money and improving nutrition. By working survival techniques into your daily routine, neither preparation nor a disaster will interrupt your life very dramatically.

CHAPTER FOUR
CANNING FOOD FOR STORAGE

Canning is an inexpensive and healthy option for preparing an emergency food supply. If you are planning for short term emergencies only, then a basic knowledge of canning will suffice. However, once you start canning, you may find yourself employing your new-found skills more than you expected.

Pressure Canning

PREPARE JARS – Wash them thoroughly, checking the rims for nicks or chips. If you find a defective jar, throw it away! Do not even attempt to use it. Unlike water bath canning, which simply involves boiling the closed jars, the jars do not need to be sterilized, or even hot, for pressure canning.

PREPARE LIDS AND RINGS – Always use new lids – the circular piece that lays inside the rings. Lids do not need anything done to them. Wash the rings thoroughly and set aside.

PREPARE FOOD – Wash, peel, slice, and snap fruits and vegetables as desired. To avoid brown fruit, soak in salt water or other type of 'fruit fresh' while you are preparing the jars. This is not necessary to the nutritional value or flavor of the fruit – it just keeps it pretty. Peaches and pears do not need to be peeled. The processing will make skins very thin and palatable. Peaches can be canned whole, without removing the pit, if desired. I do this when my peaches are too small to mess with. There is no preparation for meat unless you are canning a recipe that calls for it to be cooked or seasoned.

Some foods can be canned in a simple, large soup pot. This is called "water bath canning," but make sure it is safe for your recipe, as foods that are low in acid need to be pressure canned to be properly preserved.
(Photo credit to thebittenword.com on Flickr)

PREPARE FRUIT SYRUP – Cover fruit with Light to Heavy Syrup. The lightness of the syrup is determined by the amount of sugar added to the water. The less sugar, the lighter the syrup. To make the syrup, add the required amount of sugar to a pot of water and bring to a boil.

Use the following chart to determine a light or heavy syrup.

SYRUP CONTENT	QUART WATER	QUART SUGAR	PINT WATER	PINT SUGAR
Very Light	1½ Cups	¼ Cup	¾ Cup	⅛ Cup
Light	1½ Cups	⅜ Cup	¾ Cup	³⁄₁₆ Cup
Medium	1½ Cups	½ Cup	¾ Cup	¼ Cup
Heavy	1 ½ Cups	⅝ Cup	¾ Cup	⁵⁄₁₆ Cup

FILLING THE JARS – Fruits should be covered with a syrup. Vegetables are generally covered with plain water, with a teaspoon or so of salt added. Meat is placed in the jars raw. For ground meat, just smush it in! For chunked meats, cover with water or broth.

Fill the jars to within an inch of the top of the jar. Slide a butter knife around the inside of the jar, gently nudging the food, to release air bubbles. If air bubbles are allowed to remain, the air may cause the jar to break under the pressure of processing. Wipe the rims of the jars with a clean cloth to remove food debris and/or liquid. Place the lid on the rim of the jar and secure with the ring. Then, place the jars in the pressure canner, adding about 2 inches of water to the bottom of the canner. Set the canner lid on appropriately, and begin the process as determined by the amount and type of food being canned.

The following chart comes from a brochure published by Montana State University and outlines processing times for a variety of foods. For details on the full brochure, see the Resources section in the back of the book.

PROCESSING TIMES AND PRESSURES FOR PRESSURE CANNERS

For Select Low-Acid Vegetables, Meats and Poultry

TABLE 1. Minutes to Process.

VEGETABLES	PINT	QUART
See MT200906HR for processing times for fruits, tomatoes and mixtures		
Asparagus, spears or pieces, raw or hot pack	30	40
Beans or peas, shelled, dried, hot pack only	75	90
Beans, baked (see Beans, dry)		
Beans, dry, with tomato or molasses sauce, hot pack only	75	90
Beans, fresh lima – shelled, raw or hot pack	40	50
Beans, snap and Italian – pieces, raw or hot pack	20	25
Beets, whole, cubed, or sliced, hot pack only	30	35
Carrots, sliced or diced, raw or hot pack	25	30
Corn, cream style, hot pack only	85	NA*
Corn, whole kernel, raw or hot pack	55	85
Mixed vegetables, hot pack only	75	90
Mushrooms, whole or sliced, hot pack (½ pint same as pint)	45	NA*
NOTE: Wild mushrooms cannot be canned safely.		
Peas, green or english, shelled, raw or hot pack	40	40
Peppers, hot pack only (½ pint same as pint)	35	NA*
Potatoes, sweet, pieces or whole, hot pack only	65	90
Potatoes, white, cubed or whole, hot pack only	35	40
Pumpkin and winter squash, cubed, hot pack only	55	90
Spinach and other greens, hot pack only	70	90
Squash, winter, cubed (see Pumpkin)		

MEATS	PINT	QUART
See MT200903HR for more information on canning meat, poultry and fish.		
Chicken or rabbit, cut up, without bones, raw or hot pack	75	90
Chicken or rabbit, cut up, with bones, raw or hot pack	65	75
Ground or chopped meat, hot pack only	75	90
Strips, cubes or chunks of meat, raw or hot pack	75	90
Meat stock (broth), hot pack only	20	25
Fish, raw pack only	100	NA**
Smoked fish	110***	NA*

Directions for canning in quart jars are not available.

Directions for canning in quart jars are not available in this Montguide. See Additional Resources, page 4, **So Easy to Preserve, 5th edition only, and the USDA Home Guide to Canning, 2006 edition only, for more information on canning fish.*

***Safely canning smoked fish in pints requires distinctly different directions for filling pressure canner than for pressure canning other foods. See Montguide MT200903HR for directions for filling the pressure canner for processing smoked fish as well as the additional resources listed on page 4.*

After the processing is complete and all of the pressure has left the canner, you may open the lid. Remove the jars using a jar lifter – they will be very hot! (If you do not have another batch that needs to go into the canner, you can let them cool in the canner itself.) Set the jars on a towel on the counter. Be sure they are not in the path of cold air, such as the draft from an air conditioner vent.

Do **NOT** push the little button down! You will want to — I promise — but do not. It is essential that the jar seals on its own. As the jar seals, you will hear a pop — that is music to a canner's ear! Wait until the jar is completely cool before wiping off the sides and placing on the shelves. To keep everything organized, write the date (and contents, if necessary) on the top of the lid. If the center button has not gone down, eat the food for dinner tonight, or place the jar in the freezer to be used as soon as is convenient for your menu plans.

If you are not sure the jar is sealed, tap on the lid after it is completely cool. If it rings with a hollow sound, it is not sealed. If it rings "tight," it is. Another test is this: hold the jar by the lid (without the ring) at an inch or two off of the surface of your counter. A sealed lid will hold the weight of the jar. If the lid pops off, it was not sealed.

Bulk Canning for Emergency Preparedness

Consider the possibility of canning anything you make. These recipes are easy to make in bulk and can ahead of time, and later on in Chapter 10, we will put it all together in a simple meal plan for a month's worth of eating. Most recipes of this nature call for 90 minutes of processing at 10 pounds of pressure in quart jars, but always follow the instructions for your pressure canner.

Chili

10 pounds ground meat (any kind will do)
10 envelopes chili seasoning (consider buying 5 extra cheap ones and 5 really good ones, unless you have a favorite homemade chili mix!)
20 cups beans
5 quarts tomatoes

Brown the meat just enough to make it "mixable." Once the chili is put together – the meat does not need to be cooked through – place in quart jars and process.

Tip: Double or triple bulk recipes to make it worth your while. You may spend a day canning, but during a crisis, you'll be grateful that the hard work has already been done.

Taco Soup

One #10 can of corn
2 quarts canned or stewed tomatoes
2 quarts canned beans
5 envelopes of taco seasoning, or a homemade mix.

Mix ingredients together and process.

BBQ Hamburger

8 pounds ground meat
2 cups chopped onion
28 oz. bottle ketchup
2 cups water
1 cup chopped celery
½ cup lemon juice
4 tbsp. brown sugar
2 tbsp. Worcestershire sauce
2 tbsp. salt
4 tsp. vinegar
1 tsp. dry mustard (or 1 tbsp. prepared mustard)

Mix all ingredients and process.

Taco Meat

6 pounds ground meat
8 medium potatoes, diced
32 ounces tomato sauce
32 ounces water
2 cups chopped onion
1 tsp. ground cumin

Combine ingredients and process.

*Tip: Process some pint jars –
they make excellent instant snacks!*

Meat Loaf

6 pounds ground meat
2 cups cracker crumbs
8 beaten eggs
32 ounce tomato sauce
1 cup finely chopped onion
8 tbsp. chopped green pepper
Dash dried thyme
Dash dried marjoram

Mix ingredients, put in quart jars and process. The finished product will not be very pretty, but it will be convenient.

Beans and Wieners

One #10 can of dry beans, cooked, then lightly drained
1 – 64 oz. bottle ketchup
3 tablespoons onion salt
2 ½ cups brown sugar
3 tablespoons mustard
4 packages hot dogs

Mix ingredients together and process. It is important to cook the beans prior to processing because they will swell during cooking. If that happens during processing, the jars will break. This will yield approximately 1 dozen quart jars.

Tip: Beans are so easy to can in bulk. If your garden is too small to produce a lot of fresh beans at once, supplement with bounty from the local Farmer's Market or trade with a friend who gardens.

Try not to let bulk canning overwhelm you. One huge batch of a recipe can yield many jars. Make sure you get a pressure canner large enough to make light work. (Photo Credit to boboroshi on Flickr)

Calico Beans

1 pound ground meat, browned (consider sausage)
½ pound cooked bacon (optional)
1 cup chopped onion
1 can kidney beans, undrained
1 can butter beans, undrained
1 can pork 'n beans, undrained
1 cup sugar, brown or white
1 tablespoon vinegar
1 tsp. dry mustard (or 1 tablespoon prepared mustard)
½ cup ketchup

Variation:
Use a bag of "combination beans." They add a nice variety and save money.

Combine all ingredients and place in crock pot. Simmer on low all day, then process once cooked.

Ham N' Beans

Make a big pot of ham and beans like you ordinarily would. Eat your fill for dinner that night with a batch of homemade corn bread (that hopefully you already had in the freezer!). Process the rest as needed, then bring a jar out on a cold winter day next year.

Variation:

After the beans are soft, add some canned tomatoes, sauce or juice. It adds a nice zest!

Vegetable Soup

From Robin: I use V-8 juice and water as the base, with perhaps some chicken or beef bouillon for added flavor. Then, just throw in a bunch of fresh vegetables – frozen corn, carrots, celery, onion, potatoes – whatever you want. This is where the work is, in chopping all the veggies. Of course, you can add chunks of meat or ground meat. Once it's all put together, however, you do not have to cook the meat or the vegetables through. They will cook while the cans process.

CHAPTER FIVE
STORING DRY FOODS

Most emergency preparedness food plans rely heavily on dry food. The reason is simple: dried foods are easy to store for long periods of time. Foods like wheat, beans and rice can be obtained and stored in a variety of ways. They can be purchased in bulk and put in smaller containers at home. They can be purchased in air-tight buckets. They can be purchased in smaller, #10 cans, already sealed for long-term storage. Dry foods are extremely convenient and should be high on your priority list for developing a home store.

Finding a place to store your dry goods can be fun. Two or three cases of canned goods, with a pretty piece of material over them, make a sturdy end table. Don't have money for a box spring under a mattress? Make one out of buckets of wheat! Think outside of the box a bit, and you will find no shortage of space.

Storing and Managing Protein Sources

Have you ever heard of protein poisoning? We hadn't, either! Protein poisoning is a condition that is not uncommon in long term survival situations. We've been talking about short and long term power outages, but when Survival Spot had vegetable oil high on its list of 100 Things That Disappear First in a National Emergency, I wondered about the reason for its urgency. Oil is not high on many priority lists for food storage, especially if you don't fry foods often. If you are like us, popcorn is our biggest drain on oil, and popcorn certainly is not a requirement for survival or a major necessity for an average power outage. However, should we be faced with a very long term national emergency that would literally require us to "live off the land," protein poisoning is something to be aware of, and oil plays a major part in this.

Some rural people *(and I admit, I have been one of these – Robin)* tend to think that, in a worst case scenario, we can always rely on rabbits and squirrels to keep us alive. Rabbits are the leanest meat there is, and most other game meats are very low in fat content. In good times, we consider that a good thing. But in bad times, we desperately need that fat. If we eat a diet of only low-fat meat, we can actually starve to death with a belly-full of food. Thus, the great need for oil and fats. So, what can we do to prepare for this – admittedly, remote but serious — possibility?

RAISE YOUR OWN LIVESTOCK By raising your own livestock, you can collect and save the fat in the meat. You can render the lard at home. This added bit of fat to your diet can make the difference between life and death. However, if we are talking about a major, long-term national emergency, consider how you will provide for the animals without electricity and easy access to feed stores. Don't forget water.

STOCK UP ON PROTEIN SOURCES AHEAD OF TIME Create a supply of food that has a long shelf life and stash it away. Look for freeze-dried fruits and vegetables and other proteins, such as butter powders, sour cream powders, and others. Fatty meats can be pressure canned at home, just in case.

EXPLORE YOUR BACKYARD GROCERY STORE Spend time in your own backyard looking for edible plants. Many weeds are a healthy addition to a survival diet. Cultivate them rather than killing them. Plant an edible "Weed Garden." Look for nut trees and wild berry bushes and determine if they are edible. God really has provided us with an abundance if we just look for it.

KNOW HOW TO PLANT A GARDEN Unless you live in a windowless apartment, you have room to plant a garden. You might have to till up your pretty front yard, but at least make sure you know how to do that and have the tools and seeds necessary should it be required for survival. Even those in apartment complexes can learn how to use patios and container gardening. One very important thing to know: hybrid seeds will not produce viable seeds for the next growing season. It is imperative that you keep a supply of heirloom seeds on hand if you are preparing for long-term survival.

STORE OILS PROPERLY Storing cooking oils is a bit tricky since they tend to go rancid quite easily. They freeze well though, and the shelf life of oil doesn't begin until it is thawed. So, whatever you have in a freezer will last for up to a year after you thaw it for use. With this knowledge, you would not have to freeze more than you can use in a year. That might work if you will have a means to begin raising livestock at that point. To store without a freezer, keep the oil cool and dark. Select the highest quality of oil, and consider storing shortening or coconut oil instead.

You can extend the shelf life of your stored oil by adding BHT, Butylated hydroxytoluene. It is a chemical compound added to preserve freshness by working as an anti-oxidant. Survival Center says:

> *"BHT is available over the counter in the retail trade, but you have to know where to look for it. The only retail distributor of the anti-oxidant that I am thus far aware of is Twin Laboratories (TwinLab), Ronkonkoma, NY 11779. Their BHT comes in the form of 250 mg gelatin capsules. I've been able to find their product in several local health food stores. It is also available through mail order sources."*

Research goes both ways on the long term health effects of BHT, so it is wise to look into it and decide what is best for your family in this situation.

How to Store Grains

In an emergency situation, various cereal grains will go quickly. According to Survival Spot, rice, beans, and wheat are high on the list of items to disappear first. It is not a coincidence, as these are three of the most valuable foods for mere survival. While you can prepare to endure an emergency with a great deal of comfort and convenience, it is important that you have some basic survival foods on hand just in case.

Do you have access to #10 cans, with lids and a machine to seal it? Do you have access to mylar bags and a sealer? If so, and if you have the time, this is the least expensive way to buy grains.

RICE STORAGE - Rice can be ground for flour, eaten cooked by itself, or added to anything as an extender. It can be purchased in bulk at warehouse stores, such as Sam's Club. It comes in 50 pound bags for around $17. But, if you buy in a bag, you need to consider how you will store it for the long term. Rice can be frozen to prevent bugs from getting in it, but that uses valuable room in your freezer and uses energy for storage. You'll need to bug-proof it for longer term storage.

Smaller cans and jars of food can be stored right in your actively-used pantry so
that you can cycle them into your meal plan and keep your stores fresh.
(Photo Credit to Proxy Indian on Flickr)

If you want your rice already prepared for long term storage, you should look at purchasing sealed buckets. Thrive has 42-pound buckets of rice for around $49. Prepper Kitchen is roughly the same. Smaller, more manageable #10 cans are also available, but a really great resource for rice is The Church of Jesus Christ of Latter Day Saints. A case of 6 #10 cans only costs $30, and the work is all done for you.

BEANS - Where would any financially challenged family be without beans?! Beans are very versatile and extremely easy to can. Place one cup of dry beans in a quart jar, add one teaspoon of salt, and fill the jar with water. After putting the lids on, turn the jars upside to sit for a day or overnight. As the beans soak, they swell. When the jars are returned to an upright position, it dislodges any beans that may have become pressed together during the swelling process. At this point, process them as required.

For taco beans, add an envelope of taco seasoning, or any seasoning of your choice, when you first place the beans in the jars. After processing, the taco beans can be used as refried beans or blended smooth to use for taco pizza or bean burritos. Bean recipes such as black beans and rice, Boston baked beans, or beans and wieners can all be canned as a future convenience food.

Pinto beans are the most common bean for long term storage, although they are just one of a myriad of bean varieties available. Pinto beans can be purchased at a warehouse store for about $38 for 50 pounds. They will come in a bag, so you need to consider how you will store it for the long term. If a bucket is just too much for your small family, you can pick up smaller sizes, but they are hard to beat for an all-purpose food.

Beans can be sprouted, cooked, or ground for a flour. They can also be planted should you need to replenish your supply.

Black Beans and Rice

1 medium onion, chopped
1 tablespoon oil
1 can stewed tomatoes
1 can black beans, undrained
Variations: Used stewed tomatoes with chilies for extra zing
½ tsp. oregano
½ tsp. garlic
1½ cups rice, cooked

Cook onion and oil until tender. Add tomatoes, beans, oregano and garlic. Boil. Stir in cooked rice. Simmer 5 minutes. Let stand 5 minutes.

WHEAT STORES - Wheat is very versatile and highly nutritious. It can be sprouted and used for fresh greens. It can be cracked, baked, or ground for a variety of breads and flours. It can be planted to re-establish your supply, should the disaster last that long (Gee, I hope not!). It can even be chewed as-is. It is recommended to store as much as 200 pounds per person for one year.

Wheat Berries can be sprouted for extra nutrition and cooked into pilafs and porridges or ground into flour. (Photo Credit to cheeseslave on Flickr)

If you want your wheat already prepared for the long term, you should look at purchasing sealed buckets. A Thrive bucket of hard red wheat holds 42 pounds and costs around $49. A similar sized bucket from Prepper Kitchen is similarly priced. Buckets can be opened and resealed in between uses. If a bucket is just too much for your small family, wheat can be purchased in #10 cans that hold around 5 pounds. The least expensive resource for wheat in these smaller cans is The Church of Jesus Christ of Latter Day Saints. One case of six #10 cans is only $28! You can't go wrong!

Cooked Wheat Berries

 1 cup whole wheat berries
 2½ cups water

Place in a heavy-bottomed pan, bring to a boil. Cover partially and cook on a low boil until tender, an hour to an hour and a half. The wa-ter should cook out at the end. Season and enjoy. Adding dried cran-berries and walnuts makes a lovely pilaf.

Long-Term Storage of Sweeteners

We don't know about you, but we are not going to go through hard times without sugar! It does seem to be something that is hard to keep stocked up (probably because we keep eating it). There are many ways to sweeten stuff, such as the old unhealthy-but-yummy white sugar way, or healthier alternatives like honey, and everything in between. Sugar can be bought in bulk and stored in 40-pound pails, or bought in smaller #10 cans with a 25 year shelf life. Other sugars, like brown and powdered, can also be purchased in bulk.

Homestyle Mercantile — a family-run, home-based business — carries a Sugar Cookie Mix that would be a quick and easy way to get a sugar fix in a bad situation. They also carry healthier sweeteners, such as honey in 55 pound containers, 25 pound containers and gal-lon containers. We'll take sweeteners any way we can get them!

Are pancakes and waffles part of your emergency menu plan? They should be! But nothing is worse than bland pancakes, so you will want syrup. Homestyle Mercantile carries a maple syrup pow-der. Until you can get an order, try to stay stocked up on cheap syrup. If it gets hard, simply heat it in a double boiler just as with honey.

Fruit jellies and jams are another way to store sweeteners. You can prepare by planting an orchard now, or maybe just buy two jars of jelly every time you need to buy just one. If your orchard pro-duces, or if there is a you-pick orchard near you, you can make your own jellies. If not, just buy store-bought jelly now and then. After all, you can't plan a monthly emergency menu without including peanut butter and jelly!

To make your own applesauce, wash apples and remove the stems. Cut in half with a knife and remove the center seeds. If you have a food mill, you can skip removing the seeds. For large apples, you will want to cut them in smaller pieces for faster cooking and easier blending.

Add about an inch of water to your stockpot/Dutch oven and then place the cut apples on top. If you notice that your apples are not very juicy, you can add a little more water. I learned the hard way that by adding too much water, you end up with very watery applesauce, since the juice from the apples is basically enough liquid. Cook your apples over medium low to medium heat, checking and stirring with your wooden spoon often so your apples don't burn. Cooking times range from 30 minutes to an hour, depending on the size and juiciness of your apples. Give them a little poke with a knife from time to time. Once the knife slides through easily, they are probably cooked down enough to make into applesauce.

After your apples are cooked down, remove them from the heat and let cool a bit. A very simple prep involves just mashing the apples with a potato masher or simply mixing them with a spoon if you like chunky applesauce. Add sugar and cinnamon as desired. If you have a food mill or food processor, puree your cooked apples to the desired consistency, and add sugar and cinnamon as needed. We try not to add sugar to ours unless it is incredibly tart.

Pears are another sweet fruit, and they can well. A bit of syrup helps to preserve them and add a bit more sweetness. Stir two cups of white sugar into six cups of water in a large pot and heat over medium heat until sugar has dissolved. Turn the stove down but keep the syrup warm (just below boiling) until you are ready to add the pears. Place peeled, cored pears in a bowl of water with a generous splash of lemon juice (to prevent browning). Use a slotted spoon to lift the peeled, cored pears from the lemon water and place them in the hot syrup on the stove. Keep the pears just below a boil for five minutes in the syrup. This is called hot packing and makes it easier to place the fruit in jars. While the pears are heating in the syrup, fill your largest soup pot with water and bring to a boil. This pot should be at least as tall as your jars; ideally, the pot will be large enough that the jars can be covered with an inch of boiling water while processing.

Use the slotted spoon to transfer the pears from the syrup to sanitized jars. If you have a wide-mouthed funnel, this makes it easier to fill the jars; otherwise, just carefully slide the pears one at a time into the jar. Then use a ladle to pour syrup over the pears. The syrup should cover the pears, but leave half an inch of space at the top of the jars. Run a knife around inside the jars to remove trapped air bubbles. Wipe the rim of the jars and use a set of tongs to lift the lids from the boiling water and place them on the jars. Screw lids on tightly and process. Without a pressure canner, they should process at a rolling boil for 25 minutes.

Dried fruit is simple to make on your own and makes a wonderful snack or addition to recipes.
(Photo Credit to Vegan Feast Catering on Flickr)

Freeze-dried or dehydrated fruit is another healthy and practical way to stock up on sweets. To conquer a sweet tooth, I recommend pineapple and grapes. If you are well stocked on sugar, then you can add that to any fruits that may be a bit tart.

Let's face it. We all get a sweet tooth now and then, whether it is a healthy one or not. During a stressful time, being able to conquer that sweet tooth would be a psychological advantage – a morale booster, if you will. After the essentials are ready, consider the frills. It'll make it easier to get through tough times!

CHAPTER SIX
SHOES AND CLOTHING FOR EMERGENCIES

What clothes would make the duration of a long-term power outage more comfortable? Usually, we have a basic working wardrobe of a week or so of clothes since we have the ability to wash regularly. For extreme weather, maybe a couple of sets to play in the snow or what have you. But without the ability to wash and with the possible need to be in the elements now and then, you need a bit more than your normal wardrobe. Plan to store some clothes for each member of the family, and keep the sizes updated. Also, make a mantra of Go Large. It is easier to layer with clothes that are on the big side, and you can wear clothes that are too big easier than if the opposite is true.

Some Things to Consider

You will not have air conditioning/heat in the house. What clothing will be the most comfortable? You'll need to be able to plan for both weather extremes. In any case, you can't beat tee-shirts, sweatshirts and jeans. Most of us are practically drowning in these kinds of clothes that no one in our house wears! Tee-shirts are just about as cool as you can get if the weather is hot, but they can be layered with each other and under sweatshirts if the weather is cold.

JEANS ARE ALWAYS PRACTICAL They are protection if you are doing outside labor, like using the chainsaw or fixing a fence. They are warm, and you can stock up on leotards, tights, or long underwear to put on under the jeans. Jeans can be cut off for shorts if it is hot, but if they are your last pairs, be sure the emergency situation will be over before it gets cold!

You may be forced outside for work and/or play. What clothing will be the most functional? You'll quickly learn why people used to have "Sunday best" clothes and work clothes kept completely separate. If you find yourself outside a lot in the heat, shorts and tee-shirts are the way to go for play. Girls might even like tee-shirt dresses. That's another reason to store old shirts – you can make dresses out of them (assuming you have stocked up on needle and thread!)

If you have to work in the heat, wear large, loose, light-colored clothing. If you have to be outside in the cold, keep all skin covered against frostbite. Snow suits or work jumpers often crop up at yard sales, so grab them up. Bib overalls are good for winter, as well, because you can layer with them.

Do not over-invest in building up your supply of clothing. Keep old clothing like sweatshirts and tee-shirts rather than give them away. Watch for good buys at yard sales. You are looking for warmth or cooling, comfort, and functionality. Spring and Fall are typically mild in all areas, so you will not need special clothing for those times. Keep a priority of season-specific items first.

For winter, watch for:
- Snowsuits
- Coveralls
- Overalls
- Snow boots
- Work boots

For summer, watch for:
- Over-sized, light-colored tee-shirts
- Loose skirts that can be cooler than jeans or shorts
- Umbrellas to keep the sun off
- Wide-brimmed hats to keep the sun off

HOW WILL YOU WASH THESE CLOTHES? Wearing a tee-shirt under a sweatshirt will stall the need to wash the sweatshirt as frequently. Remember, this hypothetical situation will preclude sensitivity to cleanliness and odors. Don't worry about fashion or stains; look instead for clothes that are functional and in good shape. They don't have to match.

PLAN SIZES AHEAD - Who lives at your house now? Have an extra supply of winter and summer clothing for each of them in their current size, as well as the size they will be next year. Have a pair of walking shoes and working shoes for everyone. In case of winter, have boots that are a bit large to allow for layers of socks.

STOCK UP ON SOCKS! Socks should be worn under work boots even in the summer. I know – it's hot! But protect your feet. Keep them dry and blister free so that you can continue the work that needs to be done and to prevent a medical condition. Socks can be doubled in the winter, so, again, stock up.

You can never have enough tee-shirts. They are versatile for weather and sizes, and they can be repurposed for anything that rags can be made into.
(Photo Credit to Amy Loves Yah on Flickr)

Planning for Winter

If your area has a winter, or even a cool season, plan to store some warm clothes, focusing on layers. Tee-shirts under sweatshirts under hoodies would be very versatile, even if the house is cold. Think about clothing that dries easily, in case your family will work or play in the snow. Winter or not, you will still have chores to do.

Have clothes on hand that will be comfortable to wear while working. For example, bib-coveralls are nice for splitting wood. As you work and become warmer or need more freedom of movement, you can peel off some layers while keeping the long sleeves from the coveralls to protect the skin from frostbite.

If you have to haul water or walk somewhere for something, you will certainly want warm, sturdy boots. Find boots that are water-proof as you may be walking in snow. They should also have a good tread, as you may be walking on ice. Think about clothing and shoes that are comfortable for work, such as splitting firewood or hauling water to the house. Overall-style snowsuit pants are terrific.

At night, pajamas can be less of an issue by doubling up and putting more people in each bed. Body heat is the best heat source there is for warmth while sleeping. Hats and mittens and extra socks can be helpful, as well.

Clothing for Summer

If your area has very hot summers, plan to store some cooling clothes. Look for light colored clothing because it reflects heat. There is a reason desert-dwellers wear light colored, flowing robes.

A note from Robin - *When my husband spent two years working as a civilian in Afghanistan, he was most comfortable in very large, long-sleeved cotton tee-shirts that I was able to find at Land's End. For storage purposes, I would have just kept my eye out at thrift stores and yard sales.*

You might want to have hats on hand, as well. It is not just fashion that made southern women are known for wearing big hats – they keep the sun off the face and head. I know it sounds hot to wear a big hat in the garden, but it really will help stave off heat-exhaustion. You can find them for both men and women, and even children. Prevention is the best cure for heat exhaustion, and clothing choices will make a significant contribution.

You will be tempted to keep sandals on hand, but keep in mind that you may have to be outside more than usual, even working outside, in a power outage situation. Therefore, you will want socks and appropriate shoes, even in hot weather. If you live near a creek or other water, you might want to have a pair of worn out tennis shoes for each person so that creek play is safer. If you are in a situation where medical help will not be immediately available, it is important to prevent injuries as much as possible.

Work boots and water proof shoes are incredible important to keep your feet safe and dry while you work and travel. (Photo Credit to gumbott on Flickr)

Selecting Good Shoes

With power outages and the need to change your routine, you will likely need to walk and work outside more than usual. If you live in the woods like I do, sometimes tennis shoes are not sufficient. In a scenario where the outage or disaster stretches on long term, tennis shoes may not last long enough even if you don't live in the woods.

Keeping your habitat and possible needs in mind, each household member should have a sturdy pair of working and walking shoes – like hiking boots — with appropriate socks. They are quite uncomfortable and stiff at first, so as part of your preparation plan, plan activities where the family is wearing the boots in order to break them in. Much like clothing, it is better to have shoes that are a bit bigger than ones that are too small. Once more: don't forget the socks!

CHAPTER SEVEN
EMERGENCY SOURCES OF HEAT AND LIGHT

When disaster strikes, you quickly see what your essential needs are. Food and water are obvious needs for survival, but you may not realize just how vital a source of light and heat can be until you are without one. Think about how early in the evening the sun goes down during the winter, or how dark it can be on a stormy, heavily overcast day. You might have plenty of entertainment in the form of books, puzzles, and games, but they are of little use if you cannot see them when you sit down to play in the evening.

A heat source is more of a blatant necessity, but it might be easy to underestimate the details that go into keeping warm without power. Simply planning to start a fire is not enough; you have to be able to keep your heat source running high enough to keep the family warm and long enough to outlast the event – and that is assuming you are able to get it started in the first place.

Like any of the other areas in the home that we are preparing, it is not impossible to have good sources of heat and light ready for the what-if. It just takes a bit of planning and gathering.

An Efficient Lighting Source: Kerosene Lamps

When preparing for a long-term power outage, light is high on our personal list of priorities. Obviously, we need some light to move around our living area, but how comforting would it be to be able to read, play games, or even do needlework without electricity?

Think about what you will be doing with your lighting sources before you purchase them. Practicality rules the day when preparing for disaster!

CHOOSING LAMPS - For households without young children

or...enthusiastic...teenagers, pretty kerosene lamps are terrific. If you like antiques, it is fun to find old kerosene lamps at yard sales and auctions. You can beautify your home, indulge a hobby, and get prepared all at the same time. Need an excuse to buy pretty things at yard sales? We just provided it!

When planning for a source of lighting, think about what you will be doing after dark or before dawn. For example, if you have livestock, consider what will be the best light for you in performing your daily/evening chores. The pretty ones are nice, but they are difficult to carry outside or even around the house. They tend to be a bit top-heavy, as well, and might be dangerous if a little one bumps into the table the lamp is sitting on.

A note from Robin: I have been a fan of kerosene lamps from the beginning of my adult life. While I have never had to endure a power outage of more than 24 hours, even short outages are made more bearable by having some light. Kerosene lamps are pretty, inexpensive and practical. And, they add a touch of warmth and hominess, even romance, to any evening, with or without a storm. For these reasons, a pretty kerosene lamp is my signature wedding gift!

A practical version of a kerosene lantern is a hurricane lantern. With a handle and smaller frame, these are more portable than the prettier ones, and just as useful. I found mine in the camping section of Wal-Mart for less than $10. These will be used mainly for moving around outdoors in the dark in the event our battery supply has been exhausted.

LAMP OIL - Either of these lamps will be useless without oil! The oil for a kerosene lamp will last longer than batteries for a flashlight, but it is still consumable - hence the need to stock up. Clear lamp oil is the best because it puts out less smoke. It is less than $5 for a liter or two and is not combustible, which makes it easy to store. Pick up a bottle with each monthly grocery trip.

WICKS - If you have a lamp and you have oil, you still cannot use them without wicks. They can be purchased at your local supermarket in the candle section (which is also where you will find the oil and the pretty lamps). These, too, are consumable, so you will want to stock up on them. Or, you can stock up on the supplies to make your own.

A simple DIY wick is to soak cotton yarn in one cup of water mixed with 1 tbsp of salt and 2 tbsp boric acid. Once soaked for twelve hours and then dried, braid strands together to the appropriate thickness for your candles.

> *Tip: Wicks should fit the candle or lamp that you are making. A wick that is too small will not hold a flame, and one that is too big will cause excess smoke.*

If you find yourself in a dark situation, there is nothing like firelight to make you feel warm and cozy. Battery power is good, too, but firelight is warmer and lasts longer. Get prepared now, and if it turns out you have no need for the kerosene lamps, you will still have items that beautify your home.

A Practical Heating Source: Firewood

When you live in the woods, it is not uncommon to hear people say, "Well, you have plenty of wood in case the power is out!" That certainly appears to be the case, but the novice needs to know one very important thing: *Green wood doesn't burn very well.* So, how can you prepare firewood to last for 30 days or more and still be ready to burn at a moment's notice? You could buy it yourself from someone who has already cut and seasoned wood. Just be sure that you have enough. If you do plan to cut your own, however, there are a few important things to know.

Calculate what you need. Unfortunately, there is no "cut and dried" amount that I can say would be enough for you, if you will excuse the pun. It depends on many variables to determine how much firewood you need.

If you are heating your home with an open fireplace, you will consume more wood than a wood stove or fireplace insert. A bonfire on the ground will consume more than a cook stove. Northern Canada will require more wood than Louisiana. If you have good wood and a decent stove with a well-insulated & weather-proofed home, then the only variable is climate.

Firewood is calculated (and sold) by a volume measurement. A cord is four feet wide, four feet high, and eight feet long when stacked. A Ric is ½ of a cord. Think of a Ric as a regular pick-up bed filled level with the sides. A general rule of thumb is that a Ric should last for 30 days of eating and cooking.

CHOOSING GOOD FIREWOOD - Regardless of what kind of wood you have, firewood must be cured. This means it should be cut and left to dry out for at least 6 months. The drier it is, the better and more efficiently it will burn. Split wood cures faster and more completely than wood with only the ends cut, because the bark prevents curing. The more surface area that is exposed, the better it will burn. Additionally, hard wood burns better than soft wood. The University of Oklahoma has an excellent website that breaks down the difference between hardwoods and softwoods by BTU (measurement of heat) content. Generally speaking, oak and hickory are the best, both for BTU content and splitting characteristics. If you do not have easy access to oak or hickory, any well-cured wood will burn. Other good woods are Gum (hard to split), Maple, Elm (hard to split), Locust, Ash, Poplar, and even Willow. Sycamore is basically a water wood but will burn very fast.

A word on conifers (Cedar, Pine, etc.) – they will burn hot, but fast. Also, conifers tend to form creosote (soot) in the chimney faster than other woods, though all woods create some amount of it.

TOOLS NEEDED FOR GATHERING FIREWOOD - Tools can be as varied as time and money will allow. Think of it as the Strongarm Method vs. the Modern Era – though, when it gets down to the wire, it helps to have elements of both, as the Modern Era tools might be helpful but will require fuel as well.

This is well over a month's supply of firewood and makes a good store amount.
(Photo Credit to Gregs Landscaping on Flickr)

If you are only preparing for a 30 day power outage, the easiest way is probably to have a chainsaw and the required fuel on hand. If possible, get two chainsaws, one 18-20" for the big logs, and one, smaller, 14-16" for the branches. If you are concerned about running out of fuel for the long haul, you should also obtain a handsaw.

For splitting wood, you can get the old-fashioned kind of split-ter - an axe or maul (and be sure to practice well ahead of time), or you might rent or borrow a hydraulic splitter for a weekend to get a good bit of supply built up. That kind of work-weekend should get you enough wood for a month. A day of splitting firewood can be a fun family activity, but you have to get it done before the children become teenagers. By then, they are smart enough to know it really isn't all that fun. Don't forget the hot chocolate at the end of the day!

SAFETY CONCERNS REGARDING FIREWOOD - As part of your preparation for a crisis, learn how to use a chainsaw safely. If you find yourself cut off from the world for a couple of weeks and have a chainsaw accident...well, use your imagination! You might also want to have a pair of steel-toed boots in your stash to avoid a broken foot from a dropped log. Safety glasses are easy and cheap to obtain, and they are absolutely necessary. Again, consider the possibility of an eye injury without access to medical attention. A logger's helmet might be something to consider stashing away, as well. They come with a moveable screen to protect the eyes and face.

> *Tip: My husband was my source for this section, and he wants me to share the necessity of raising the face screen before you spit! - Robin*

For long-term chainsaw operations, ear plugs are a must! To get by for a couple of weeks, they may not be as important, but they are super cheap and certainly do not take up any space. Why not grab some while you are thinking about it? You will certainly want some heavy gloves. Blisters can become infected and, again, you need to be avoiding medical emergencies. Leg chaps are a good protection from the chainsaw, as well as from the flying debris and tree limbs.

SAFETY CONCERNS REGARDING FIRES - If you are heating your home with wood, the chimney must be cleaned at least yearly. While conifers produce the most creosote, all woods produces some, so it is very important that you do not neglect this. If you do not normally use your fireplace, be sure the chimney is clean now, before a crisis. You do not want to add a house fire to your problems in the event of a major power outage. Some homeowner's insurance providers offer a discount if you turn in your receipt for the chimney cleaning. Or, you can clean the chimney yourself.

Just for fun: I cannot say the phrase "clean the chimney" without hearing Dick Van Dyke singing *Chim Chim Cheree*.

STARTING A FIRE - Do you have a way to light the wood on fire? It seems sort of obvious, but matches can be like batteries - an afterthought! And in an emergency situation, those are not the afterthoughts you want to have. Store a supply of matches in a rodent-proof container. Mice can chew on the ends of matches and start a fire when and where you don't want them to. Be sure your matches stay dry, as well, so that they are not ruined.

Starting a fire is possible with leaves and kindling, like in the movies, but having fire starters in your stash is easier. They can also be made quite easily.

If you need to, you can block off the room where the fireplace is and just live in that area of the house to make heating more efficient.

Homemade Fire Starters

STEP ONE - Collect and save your paper egg cartons (or put out the word at church you'd like to have some, and you'll find yourself drowning in them!), and stuff each section with collected and saved lint from your dryer.

STEP TWO - Dig out the wax from used up candles (or buy paraffin wax at your local grocery store, in the canning section or by the Jello) and place it in a pot or double boiler. It does not have to be an old pot because this process will not damage it. If you do not have a double boiler, place the pot inside a larger pot that has enough water in it to cause the smaller one to float. This is a homemade double boiler. Bring the water to a boil, and this will melt the wax that is in the smaller pot.

STEP THREE - Drizzle the melted wax generously over the dryer lint in the egg carton. Let dry. Break off one section of the egg carton fire starter for each fire.

To start a fire, begin with your fire starter. Then, stack kindling – small pieces of dry wood, like twigs, small sticks and bark – around the fire starter in the shape of a teepee. Light the fire starter. When the kindling is well-lit, add some wood that is a bit larger than the kindling. When that is burning very well, you can then add a large log. If you add too many big logs too soon, your fire will go out.

CHAPTER EIGHT
SANITATION

Being without electricity for days at a time is becoming more and more common. Ice storms, tornadoes, and severe lightening strikes are part of our lives these days. Add the remote, yet not impossible, prospect of a terrorist attack, labor strike, or power station shut down, and being prepared for the worst becomes a necessary reality.

After food and water, sanitation is certainly something high on my list of priorities. I know how to potty outside – I just don't want to if I don't have to! And when feminine hygiene and diapers are thrown into the mix, things can get challenging very quickly without some advanced preparation.

Making Pottying as Pleasant as Possible

Let's start with pottying outside. Going Number #1 for boys is obviously not a problem. It is a bit more complicated for girls. Women really only have two less-than-pleasant options: squat or learn to urinate standing up.

If you choose the squatting method, you will want to prepare by strengthening your thighs. How? Simple: do squats every day, and every day do more than you did yesterday. To do so, stand with feet shoulder width apart, and — you guessed it — squat. Then stand up, and repeat. Try to keep your heels on the floor, and get as low to the ground as you can.

If exercise is not your thing, the GoGirl company makes a tool that allows women to urinate standing up. This isn't a bad gizmo to have even in good times. It is small and discreet enough to carry in your purse. If you have a problem sitting on public toilet seats, you might want to look into this no matter what.

The point here is that if you do not prepare a way to use the toilet beforehand, your only option will be to squat outside. There is really no way to make that pleasant, but if you are not in good shape, your legs will get really sore on top of everything else. And if you are going #2 . . . you had better hope your thighs are really strong!

If it is going to be just a short-term proposition, then just do the best you can. If you are faced with sanitation challenges for a longer period of time, there are a few things to consider. Avoid streams, creeks and other water sources. Dig a hole and bury your deposit, or spread it out on a rock so that it will dry and flake away, leaving less impact on the environment.

Wiping? Please know what poison ivy looks like! One tip is to save all of those phone books that we get for free. They are easy to store, and the paper inside is clean and perfect for paper wiping. It certainly sounds more pleasant than big oak leaves. Better yet, have a supply of baby wet wipes (or the ingredients to be able to make your own) stocked up.

Homemade Wet Wipes

You will need:
- 10 cup container (ex: rubbermaid, w/lid)
- ½ roll of Bounty paper towels
- 2 tbsp. of baby oil

- 2 tbsp. of baby bath
- 2 cups of water

Mix the liquid ingredients in a bowl. Set aside.

Cut the roll of paper towels in half, remove the tube, set aside.

Place half of the towel into the 10 cup container. Saturate the towels with the liquid mixture. Pull the top towel up for your starter towel. Let them sit for about an hour, or until the towels have absorbed the liquid. Put the lid on, and there you go!

> *Tip: Rags can be used in place of paper towels so that you do not have to worry about keeping a paper towel stash on hand. Wash as you do other laundry, with a few extra rinses and some vinegar to keep fresh.*

When You Don't Want to Potty Outside

I think the most practical plan is to have a way to potty inside at night, and only potty outside during the day. A variation on that is to have a way to potty at night and do Number #2 inside. Urinating outside isn't really that bad and will save on resources.

What are our other options?

- A five-gallon bucket with a seat on top. This is a great idea indoors or out, just because I don't want to do exercises to strengthen my squatting muscles!
- An inexpensive Port-A-Potty. These containers hold a lot of waster and have disposable bags and chemicals to control odor. Be sure you stock up on bags and chemicals.
- A fancy-shmansy portable toilet. This is the Cadillac! If you are in a position (no pun intended) to go with ultra convenience and comfort, do it! Personal sanitation is not an area that one needs to feel guilty about wanting to be spoiled. What a morale booster it would be to at least manage this one aspect of daily life comfortably and conveniently. All it takes is a bit of pre-planning.
- A composting toilet. There are sustainably designed toilets spe-

posables, however, they are still much more cost-effective, at about $800-1,000 per child versus >$1,500. Plus, you have the assurance of them fitting no matter what, as well as the benefit of easier storage. Still, washing is a major consideration, and these are the thickest of the cloth diapering options.

POCKET DIAPERS – Pocket diapers have a single absorbent layer and the waterproof layer, and extra absorbency is stuffed into the pocket. This makes them simple to put on the child, like all-in-ones and disposable diapers, but it cuts back on thickness for washing, as the insert is washed separately. These can be purchased in one-size options as well as sized.

> *Tip: Consider making your own cloth diapers. They can be constructed out of anything from inexpensive, thrifted fabrics such as tee-shirts and terry cloth towels, all the way up to adorable specialty fabrics. Wool and fleece covers can be affordably made from felted (shrunk) sweaters and thrifted fleece blankets.*

FITTED DIAPERS – Fitteds look and function like all-in-ones and pockets in that you simply snap or Velcro them on like a disposable. The difference is that they lack a waterproof layer and need a cover. They do tend to be a bit thicker, though not quite so much as an all-in-one, so that must be considered for washing and drying convenience.

PREFOLDS AND FLATS – These are rectangular pieces of fabric that fold around the child and are secured with pins or other measures. Flats are larger and only one layer, so they require folding before wrapping them around the child. Prefolds are just what they sound like – pre-folded – so that all you have to do is put them on and secure. They are both easier to wash than other diapers, and flats are probably the fastest to dry, since they open up to be a single layer of fabric. These are also the most cost effective, as you can buy enough for a child for just a couple hundred dollars or less.

With snapping, diaper-shaped covers, both of these diapers can simply lay inside the cover as you put it on, meaning there is no need to secure the diaper on with pins or otherwise. For extra security or when wearing them under fleece or wool pants as a cover, you need to pin them or, as many parents prefer, use a Snappi closure. This is a small, rubber gizmo with three "legs" and a claw shaped hook on each end. The claws grab the fabric of the diaper at each hip and in the center to hold the diaper securely on. It is safe and simple – much easier than trying not to poke the baby with a pin, especially if you are inexperienced with pins.

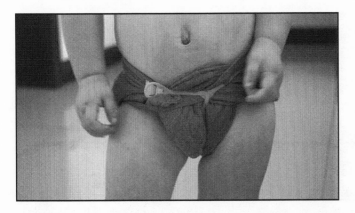

Pins and rubber pants aren't the only game in town these days. Gadgets like the Snappi pictured here make cloth diapering simple.
(Photo Credit to simplyla on Flickr)

COVERS – If your diaper selection is not waterproof, you will need to chose covers, as well. Some covers are contoured in the shape of a diaper and snap or Velcro on. They can be one-size or sized, and made out of a number of waterproof fabric options.

PUL (polyurethane lined) covers are plastic or rubbery feeling and are the thinnest and seemingly most durable of cover options. PUL also offers less "breathing" than other options, though, so if your child may be prone to allergic reactions or skin irritation, take that into consideration.

More natural fabric options include wool and fleece. The natural lanolin in wool is a water repellent, and it will wick moisture away from both skin and clothing. Fleece is not genuine wool, but it is a bit more durable, and thick enough that it will wick moisture as well. After a lot of washing, though, this waterproofing can be stripped on both fabrics, so you need a few tubes of lanolin on hand to replenish it. A common choice is lanolin used as a breastfeeding ointment, with the bonus that you can use it for that purpose as needed, as well.

Tip: To lanolize a diaper cover, squirt an inch or so of lanolin into some hot water with a teaspoon of soap, and melt the lanolin. Once it has dissolved, add it to a sink full of water and lay the covers, inside-out, in it to soak for about 30 minutes. Roll the covers in a towel to squeeze the water out, then lay flat to dry. They should remain waterproof like this for about one month.

Wool and fleece can also be made into pull-on "shorties" or pants that go right over the diaper without any other cover. This can cut down on your clothing stash, though they will need to be size-specific.

To only have to wash every few days, try to have three to four dozen diapers of any style and 4-10 covers (if needed) to make a comfortable supply for a given size. Prefolds and flats, one-size pockets, and one-size all-in-ones can be purchased in one, adjustable size for each child. You will need to take sizing needs into consideration for size-specific diapers.

Washing Cloth Diapers

Just like washing any other laundry, you will want a 5-gallon bucket and a plunger. This makes it easier to agitate the diapers for thorough cleaning. If you have a way to heat the water, you are ahead of the game. If you don't have soap, you just won't have soap and the baby will survive for a little while – though rashes might become a concern. However, the supplies for homemade laundry soap are extremely cheap and easy to store, and the soap is easy to make – even without electricity. We'll get to that in *Chapter 12*, with a homemade laundry soap recipe and general washing instructions.

Diapers are a bit more unique than regular laundry in that they get much dirtier than other clothes. While you can re-wear a shirt with a bit of dirt, you cannot reuse a dirty diaper. Covers can be extended a bit by spot-treating any poop that might leak onto them. Still, you have to get diapers thoroughly cleaned, or they will stink horribly and cause irritation.

Poop on diapers should be shaken into your potty-system or buried. Anything that remains on the diaper should wash off, though if you have the means to soak or rinse it off, it will make handwashing a bit easier. Exclusively breastfed babies make extremely easy to wash poop that doesn't need anything special done to it. It will simply rinse away. Sun-bleaching as they dry on your line will take care of any stains that might be left.

> *Tip: Securing prefolds, flats, and fitted diapers with a closure, like the Snappi, helps to keep the diaper close to their skin to prevent leaks onto the cover and into their clothes.*

To get a head start on washing, consider soaking diapers in a "wet pail" system. This would be a container filled 1/4 of the way with water, and maybe a bit of baking soda, vinegar, and/or essential oils. Throw diapers into the wet pail as they are soiled, and the stains will be loosened and even lifted before you wash. This water needs to be emptied daily, so if you would have limited water access in an emergency situation, weigh that against any benefits that might arise from easier washing.

Without a wet pail, diapers can be simply placed into a dry pail with a bit of baking soda or a waterproof bag, ironically called a "wet bag" – named because it stores wet things, not because you keep it wet like the pail.

Try not to use your full stash of diapers before washing, as it will take some time to wash them and let them dry. Washing a dozen diapers at the end of the day and letting them dry overnight is much easier than washing three dozen every few days and chancing whether you will run out before the cleaned ones dry. When purchasing your diapers, however, try not to count on daily washing, as you never know what the day may bring. You do not want to commit yourself to something that you may not be able to manage.

Pre-soaked or not, diapers do need to soak for awhile in washing water before agitation. They need to be fully wet, through and through, and that takes more than just dumping them into water. Make sure that they are opened up fully and not rolled or closed up. Pocket inserts should be removed, and flats should be fully opened up.

Submerge in your washing container with soap and water and let soak for awhile. Then agitate with a plunger or gloved hands, let the water drain out, and wring the diapers out before hanging to dry.

Feminine Hygiene in Disaster Scenarios

In 2007, the Tulsa, OK, area was hit with a major, surprise ice storm. Many people were without power for a week. In July, 2012, severe storms knocked out the power for 2 million people along the East Coast. Electricity was unavailable for more than a week for thousands. In August, 2012, 60 million people were without power for days in India – that is more people than lives in the United States and Canada combined! And what does Murphy's Law state what will happen on Day 1? Your period will start, whether it's due or not! Hopefully, you have a couple months' supply of feminine hygiene products. But if not, here are some ways you can prepare for the inevitable.

STOCK UP – Make sure you have stored a couple of month's worth of feminine products. Sanitary napkins do take up space. An easy fix for that is be prepared with tampons – even if you don't like them, they would work in a pinch and take up less space to store. Consider your options for disposing, as well, and be prepared for that.

PURCHASE WASHABLE SANITARY NAPKINS – Cloth pads are growing in popularity, and there are a variety of places to purchase them online and even in some stores. Try Pleasure Puss Menstrual Pads, Glad Rags, and Luna Pads, to name a few.

GO DIY – Make, or have the materials on hand to make, washable sanitary napkins. They are extremely inexpensive and extremely easy. They are even easy to make by hand in the event the power is already out when you need to make them! "J," writing for Wellsphere, says,

> *"Even a novice seamstress can create a basic menstrual pad from recycled items in less than a half hour! If I can do it, any-one can. I don't measure or make sure my seams are straight, because I figure something you are going to bleed on doesn't need to look pretty."*

One of the easiest ways to make a sanitary napkin is to use towels – terry cloth or microfiber – cut into rectangles roughly 3x the width of your underwear. Microfiber can be harsh on sensitive skin, so it may help to sew a strip of cotton down the very center of the towel. To use them, trifold so that the cotton strip is in the center and facing your skin. If they need to be thicker, you can double them up. The friction between the towel and underwear will help to hold them in place. The flexibility of thickness is a definite benefit, along with the ease to make them. They will also wash and dry easily, much like flat diapers. However, without a waterproof layer, you will need to pay attention to changing it to avoid leaks.

Another way to make a sanitary napkin is to trace your favorite disposal, leaving an inch or so for seam and turning allowance, then use it as a template to cut out a few layers of cotton, terry cloth, and fleece. Sew around the edges, leaving an opening so that you can turn it inside out – or outside in, as the case may be. Sew the open-ing closed, and you have a menstrual pad. Adding a bit of stitching around the inside will give it some shape and help to prevent frustrating run-off, though that certainly is not necessary. These will be more leakproof, giving you the possibility of longer wear, but it will take longer to wash and dry due to the layers.

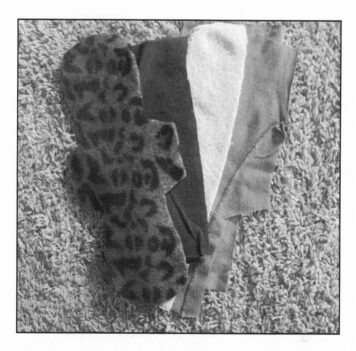

An extra-absorbent pad can be made from two layers of tee-shirt fabric, two layers of flannel, and one layer each of microfiber and fleece. Stack them so that the fleece and flannel will be on the bottom and the tee-shirt will be facing your skin. Wing shapes are optional. Either stack them in order and serge around the edges, or invert them, sew around leaving a small opening, then turn right-side out and stitch the opening closed.

Washable sanitary napkins should be part of preparedness storage for another reason: laundry. By wearing a napkin routinely, it will absorb normal odor and moisture, making it possible to wear even underwear an extra day before washing. It can extend the amount of time you need to wash jeans by several days. If all else fails, simply use the prefolds you have on hand, or any rag or towel.

TRY A MENSTRUAL CUP – Menstrual cups are used internally, like tampons, but rather than absorbing the fluids, it collects into a flexible cup, which you can remove and empty. Reusable cups like the Diva or Keeper will need to be rinsed, but it only takes a bit of water that you can pour from a cup or bottle. Disposable cups like the Instead do not need to be rinsed, but they are not as durable, reliable, or reusable. While reusable cups cost a bit more than the others, you only need one per person, and it will last for a long time. There is a bit of a learning curve, and a backup pad is a good idea at least for awhile. No matter what, though, it will cut back on your pad usage — and therefore your need to wash. As a bonus that would be quite helpful in this scenario, women often comment that they notice a difference in their flow and an improvement in cramps and other discomfort when they switch to cloth pads or menstrual cups.

Whether there is a power outage, a natural disaster, or a nation-wide collapse, bodily function will continue to, well, function. With a little bit of forethought and preparation, we can make those natural occurrences as pleasant and comfortable as possible.

CHAPTER NINE
BUYING SUPPLIES

Once you are in good shape with food, water, heat and clothing for one month, it's time to start branching out. Just in case our hypothetical situation goes much longer than anticipated, you will find yourself having to be very resourceful. Remember that necessity is the mother of invention. What do you have laying around that can be useful? What would that look like if you were to begin making intentional purchases? Since you are now preparing for you-don't-know-what, be creative. Be resourceful ahead of time. What items can you never have too much of?

Start with items that are geared towards survival. Look for things that will contribute to cooking, warmth, staying dry or creating some time of energy. Start to look for items that you will need to function.

- WD-40 - Lubricates anything; useful if you have rarely used machinery.
- Duct Tape - What CAN'T you do with duct tape? Repair boots; bind splints on a broken bone; repair a tent.

- Rope - Use to make temporary shelter; clothesline inside or out; tie things down; jump rope.
- Bungee Cords - Hold things down.
- Tarps - Put on the ground to keep firewood (or anything else) from becoming damp; build a temporary cover or shelter; cover a damaged roof after a storm; cover firewood to protect it from rain; line a wooden container to hold water.
- Used bicycles, working or not - Use to build a pulley system; use as a stationary bike to generate energy for grinding grains or re-charging batteries; use as exercise to prepare to be physically fit.

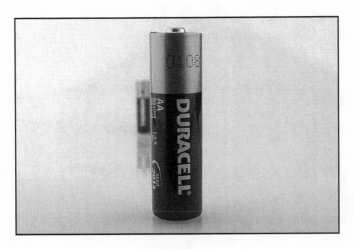

Keep record of anything you store that will need batteries and what kind – then be sure to stock a sufficient supply of each.
(Photo Credit to Anton Fomkin on Flickr)

Your last priority is convenience and comfort.

- Super Glue - Seal minor cuts (be very certain the cut is VERY clean) or to seal small leaks;
- Blue Dawn Dishwashing Soap - Kills fleas on contact; make ice bag (fill freezer bag with it and put in freezer); repel ants; wash poison ivy rash;
- Paper/Pens - Leave notes; teach a child to write; send a letter the old-fashioned way; start a fire; draw a map

As with all preparations, do not go into debt. Work within your budget to add a little bit to your preparedness plan each week, month or payday. Yard sales and what you might find there are not at all predictable. So, allot an amount to be spent at yard sales and resale shops. Keep this in cash in your purse (but only if you are very disciplined! This is not soda pop money!).

Be creative! Buy stuff - used if possible - that you just know might help. Talk to your spouse and housemates. They will approach this from a different point of view. Look for stuff to keep motors running, stuff to make household repairs, stuff to repair fences and animal pens. If you think practically about it, being a pack rat can be a good thing.

What to Look For at Yard Sales

Yard sales, resale shops, Craigslist, and hand-me-downs can be a treasure trove if you know what you are looking for when you go. Unlike walking into the store with a grocery list, you cannot necessarily know what will be there when you set out. However, if you have an idea of what you need – or a list – you can grab it when you see it rather than wondering whether it is a necessity or, worse, missing out on a deal because you forgot you needed it.

CLOTHING - Keep an eye out for blue jeans, tee-shirts, sweatshirts, shoes and socks. None of these have to fit well or be pretty. Just look for something sturdy and serviceable. Remember that nearly all durable clothing can be repurposed, as well. Jeans can be made into blankets, shirts into rags and diapers. If you get something and find that it wasn't something you needed after all, or your kid grows out of it before you need it, consider reusing it for something else. Or, you can return the favor of that great deal and pass it along to another family.

BUCKETS – especially 5-gallon buckets. These can be used for so many things: toilets, water, washing clothes, washing dishes, and the list goes on. If you plan to store food in buckets, make sure they are food grade and very clean before using them.

RAGS - Pick up anything that can be used as rags. This might include tee-shirts with holes in them, well-worn sheets and pillow cases, cloth diapers, and thin towels. As an added benefit, rags can be made into various things, too. You can never have enough rags.

> *Tip: Tee-shirts and rags can be cut into long, continuous strips and then twisted into rope. While it can be done by hand, try putting the ends of two strands into a power drill, where the bit would go. Have another person tightly hold the strips fully extended, and let the drill twist the strands. Fold the twisted strands in half so that it rolls into itself, then do it again. It will continue to twist onto itself and form surprisingly strong rope.*

BLANKETS - Any blanket that will provide warmth or can be used to sleep on outside is serviceable. Sleeping bags can usually be found pretty easily. Blankets can be layered if they are too thin to use singly, so don't pass them by on that merit.

CLOTH DIAPERS AND COVERS - Even if you do not use cloth diapers now, in a power outage that lasts longer than your supply of disposables, you will be glad you have them. If you do not currently have a child in diapers, it is possible a child could be stranded with you. And, they serve double duty as rags and cleaning cloths as well.

BOOKS AND BOARD GAMES - After a few hours of having no electricity, the novelty wears off. But, if you have a stash of good books and games, you can keep the fun going for the duration. Get books at all reading levels, as well as books that make good overall read-alouds. When purchasing games, do not get anything that requires batteries! Unless you want to stock up on batteries, that is.

KEROSENE LAMPS - As mentioned earlier, in Chapter 7, these can serve an excellent purpose for efficient lighting, and they are often seen in yard sales and thrift shops.

CANNING JARS - Canning use aside, half-pint jars are perfect, absolutely perfect, for safely carrying votive candles around the house. Even little children can manage them without danger of knocking them over because of their wide, stable bases. Quart jars are good for storing drinking water.

DENIM JEANS - Storing a supply of denim is nice for more than just wearing pants. It also makes an easy-to-assemble and very warm blanket material. Even if you do not quilt or sew, it is easy to cut squares of denim and sew them together by hand into a blanket. What could be more durable and versatile than a denim blanket? If you do not have batting material and need a thicker blanket, just tie two (or three!) together with yarn.

BUNGEE CORDS AND TARPS - You can never have too many! The things you might find to use these for are endless.

GAS STORAGE CANS - Gas is difficult to store, but if you have a generator, you are going to need fuel. Why buy new? Do be sure used fuel cans are safe before purchasing them.

CRAFT SUPPLIES - A menagerie of assorted bits of craft supplies can keep children, and restless adults, busy for hours. There is nothing like having no electricity to bring out our creative sides!

Keep the yard sale shopping checklist from *Appendix B* close at hand for easy "prepping" shopping when you're out and about at flea markets and garage sales.

In Fantasyland: Top of the Line Resources

It can be so expensive and impractical to dream big that I will only have the perfect off-grid home in Fantasyland. Still, one amazing thing about survival preparation is that it can double as "off-grid" living, and vice versa. If you are looking toward making long-term provisions or making this part of your lifestyle, it cannot hurt to set your sights a bit higher, if only for a dream.

KITCHEN COOKSTOVE - Wood burning kitchen cookstoves make cooking and baking without power much more convenient – especially if you have it installed right into the kitchen. You can find them new for $3,000 and up, but Angela's in-laws found one at an estate auction for under $500 and now use it almost exclusively when cooking from October to May. Using the woodstove means free fuel from downed trees or wood cut from around the property, and no more propane stove. Their one tank of propane has now lasted them more than a year and a half without needing to be refilled.

Another option is an oven that attaches to the exhaust pipe of your woodstove for heating. These are $500 or so new. The thought of sitting by the fire with fresh bread and cookies in the oven make a winter power outage sound rather cozy.

REFRIGERATOR - While it still takes a fuel source for power, natural gas and propane refrigerators are an option. This would be a great convenience if you had the energy source instead of relying only on the stability of the grid for power.

There are also interesting contraptions available through the Amish that allow you to convert horse power (literally, a horse walking on an energy-producing treadmill device) into power capable of working a cooling device. This could be used for both freezing and refrigeration in a power-outage situation!

A note from Angela – While these tools are a bigger investment, being able to switch completely from dependence on a strained electric grid to reusable, renewable, and locally-based power is freeing. And for long-term survival situations, it would be invaluable to have uninterrupted refrigeration no matter what is going on.

COMPOSTING TOILET - This is what I call surviving! How much better would it be to have a real toilet than to potty out in the woods? Composting toilets flush waste with little to no water to a unit that decomposes and evaporates waste into removable compost. The more expensive options ($3-5k range) look like the toilets you are familiar with and have fewer restrictions. Considering the alternative of using a bucket, it seems strange to say "base model," but the base models can be purchased in the $2k range. If you are looking for long term sustainability, this could be a worthwhile investment. Don't forget to look at composting and treatment aids when you are preparing your supplies.

WOOD HEATER - We have a fireplace insert at our house, and it kicks out a lot of heat. Two problems I offer so that you can try to avoid them in your own planning:

First, we have no way to vent the heat to circulate it through the house. But since we are in Fantasyland – we would put one in every major room!

A note from Angela – The house we are going to be purchasing has their single wood heater tied into the central heat air ducts with a custom sootless system. They paid $1000 in labor and supplies to have it done and, because it's connected to the main system, the thermostat for the Central Heat system will only kick on when the temperature drops. This system overcomes the primary problem with wood heaters – heating one room to a thousand degrees while other rooms remain freezing cold.

The second problem we have is that I have very little space to cook anything on the fireplace insert and no way to bake anything. I can only heat or cook something in a small pan, and right now, it's not enough for the six adult-sized people living in my house. This would be the benefit of a having wood-burning cookstove over a regular fireplace.

OFF-GRID LAUNDRY TOOLS - While the plunger method is rather inexpensive and very efficient, light washing could be simplified quite a bit with a Wonderwash. These are hand-cranked tumblers that make light work of light washing. At around $50, they aren't too much of a fantasy, either!

For more of an investment, including the fuel to power them, propane washers and dryers are available, as well, meaning they would be able to handle bigger loads and tougher washes – and you wouldn't have to change your routine a bit!

This little visit to Non-Electric, Off-Grid Fantasyland has been a blast, and maybe, someday, we'll have whole houses prepared for any emergency...but we're not holding our breath. For now, baby steps will be enough.

SECTION III
PREPARING FOR ACTION

"Action springs not from thought, but from a readiness for responsibility."

Dietrich Bonhoeffer

CHAPTER TEN
MENU PLANNING FOR A MONTH

The last two years have shown us major, nationwide droughts. That will translate into rising food costs and, possibly, impending food shortages. This could mean we will have to live out of our own pantry for a month. Temporary layoffs and disabilities could also make it necessary to live out of your pantry. And, as always, there is the possibility of a major power outage lasting two or three weeks. How much peace of mind would it give you to be 100% self-sufficient for one month when that first ice storm is predicted?

With busy lives, jobs, and schools, it is often challenging to figure out what is for dinner tonight, let alone make a menu for a week. Planning for a whole month can be completely overwhelming. But don't let that keep you from starting. How about starting with this question: How much does one person eat in a month?

Taking a Food Shortage
One Month at a Time

The Food Guys make it very easy to see exactly what your family needs for one month. Via their website, simply tell them how many people are in your household, then divide the totals by 12. As you will see, a 30-day supply of food is not very much.

For example, one person needs about 25 pounds of grain to last one month. This grain can be in several varieties – wheat, rice, cornmeal, pasta, etc.

A note from Robin: I focus a lot on wheat for several reasons. It is sproutable, it is extremely nutritious, it is versatile, and it grinds into flour. Plus, our family doesn't like rice all that much.

Here is what The Food Guys recommend for grains, per person, for 30 days, but remember to stock what your family will eat:

Wheat	12.5 pounds
Flour	2 pounds
Cornmeal	2 pounds
Oats	2 pounds
Rice	4 pounds
Pasta	2 pounds
	25 pounds total

PROTEIN - This can span legumes, canned meat, and TVP (Textured Vegetable Protein). The Food Guys' recommendation for legumes is 5 pounds total, including 1/2 pound of dry soup mix. Meat amounts will depend on your family's preferences and needs.

Dried beans are a great source of necessary protein, and some can be sprouted for extra nutrition or replanting, as well. (Photo Credit to FatherJack on Flickr)

DAIRY - For dairy, they recommend six pounds, including one can of evaporated milk, as well as butter, sour cream, cheese, etc., as desired. If you do not drink much milk, the amounts can remain the same, simply weighted toward other forms of dairy.

SWEETENERS - I refuse to be stranded without sweets! A 30-day supply is only 5 pounds for the average family. If you take into account honey, molasses, jelly/jam, etc., it isn't hard to stock up on enough for everyone.

PRODUCE - I had a rough time with fruits and veggies. The Food Guys recommend 15.5 pounds each for one person for 30 days. That sounds like so much! Also, one must store freeze-dried or dehydrated fruits and vegetables in preparation for some kind of emergency. Freeze-dried and dehydrated fruits and vegetables don't weigh very much, so we attempted the math. *(WARNING: Double check for your own family!)* We think we figured out that one #10 can each of freeze dried fruits and vegetables is what one person needs for 30 days.

FATS AND OILS - You probably have a 30-day supply on hand already. The Food Guys only recommend 2 pounds, and that includes shortening, oil, peanut butter, and salad dressing.

MISCELLANEOUS - Some items are used in such miniscule amounts that you can easily store what you need for a full year.

Baking Powder - 1 pound

Baking Soda - 1 pound

Yeast - ½ pound

Salt - 5 pounds

Vinegar - ½ gallon

With it broken down, you can see that it isn't as hard or expensive as it sounds to stock up for only one month. When that's done, you can work on the second month, if you'd like. My ultimate goal is 1+ years.

As a recap, here are some other necessities to have on hand for the month:

- Water - 14 gallons per person for two weeks; 1 gallon of bleach *(Chapter 2)*
- Something to cook with – seasoned firewood, propane stove *(Chapter 3, Chapter 7)*
- Something to cook in – appropriate pans and tools *(Chapter 3)*
- A menu plan to make cooking outside as easy as possible *(Coming up in this chapter!)*
- A way to clean up *(Chapter 8)*
- One month of diapers and wipes *(Chapter 8)*
- One month of feminine hygiene supplies *(Chapter 8)*
- Contraception - Will you be exposing yourself to pregnancy during these 30 days, and do you want a baby nine months from now? *(Chapter 14)*
- Medical supplies – might you have to stitch somebody up or a need to administer antibiotics or pain medications? Are you on

a regular prescription? Talk to your doctor about having an extra month's worth in storage as part of your prepping plan. *(Chapter 14)*

- A lighting source for each member of the family. *(Chapter 7)*
- A way to go potty as comfortably as possible. *(Chapter 8)*
- Morale boosters: candy, books (non-electronic!), games, etc. *(Chapter 9)*

With a list like this, your family could be completely isolated for 30 days and do just fine. Now, you just need to be ready to implement it.

Building a 30 Day Emergency Menu Plan

Once you have your food stored for the month, when it comes down to it, what would you cook? Twenty-five pounds of grain and a bunch of beans are one thing, but the trick is being able to convert that into meals your family likes and will eat. **Assuming you are prepared enough to have water and a heat source**, here are some suggestions to develop thirty day's worth of meals for your family. Adjust and adapt to your family as desired.

ENTREES - Starting with entrees is wise because they are the heartiest of your meals and will go the farthest. Of course, home canning is one option. The work is done ahead of time, and then it is very convenient on eating day. A variation on that theme requires you to be able to cook the meal on eating day. The best method I've seen is the 52 Method. In this case, the meals are still pre-canned with a shelf-life of several years, but they are uncooked. You put them together dry, add an oxygen absorber, and then cook on eating day.

Using this method, if your recipe calls for meat, then you need to obtain freeze-dried meat so that it will maintain its shelf life. Casseroles and soups are good options for this method. Most soups use dry rice or dry pasta, which can easily be added to the jar, along with the appropriate dry seasonings, freeze-dried or dehydrated vegetables, and powdered broth.

When it comes time to cook, just add the contents of the jar to a pot of boiling water. This is a terrific variation and much easier on processing day, but you will need to have a heating method to prepare it on eating day. By spending the time and energy up front on processing day by, well, processing everything, each meal is already cooked. When eating day rolls around, you will have no need for a heat source because the meal can be eaten directly out of the jar, although it will be at room temperature.

PREPARED ENTREES – canned soups and such – are an option you might want to take a look at if you are short on time. They are more expensive than the 52 Method, but there is absolutely no labor involved. Our time is worth more than we think!

BREAKFASTS - With a heat source, be it a camp stove or open fire, you can purchase a griddle and make pancakes or scrambled eggs. The pancake mix can be from scratch – use egg powder to compensate for the lack of fresh eggs during a power outage – or it can be a prepared mix.

On top of that, I just learned that hot cereals can be pressure canned. Cook the cereal as usual, in water, using the slow-cook variety. Add fruits, sugars, spices, etc., to your liking and process. I would definitely use pint jars for this one. Also consider just simply buying a supply of canned fruits and apple sauce to use for breakfast items during a long power outage. You could also preserve your own fruit juices. Take note of your cooking options and plan around them. For example, you won't have the toaster, but will you have a griddle to "toast" bread on?

INDIVIDUAL INGREDIENTS - By keeping a supply of main ingredients on hand, you can put together most of your family's favorite recipes even without electricity. Some things that you should consider for long-term storage are pastas, sauces in jars (tomatoes are highly acidic and eventually rust through tin cans), onions, peppers and celery. All of these can be purchased in freeze-dried form, with their freshness and nutrition intact. Egg powder, butter powder, sour cream powder and powdered milk are other staples that you might want to think about. Home canned meat or freeze-dried meat are also good items to have on hand.

DESSERT - Do yourself and your family a favor and have a dessert on hand. It is possible to get dessert mixes with a long shelf-life that only use water. The only two practical reasons to invest in a dessert in this form are a) you don't have to store fresh eggs or oils and b) it will stay fresh on your shelf for years. For impractical reasons, consider that you can add brownies, macaroons or ice cream as potential desserts for long-term storage in this form.

A note from Robin: Without heat and water, I have to recommend ice cream as my favorite – yep, freeze-dried ice cream! What a terrific morale booster! Freeze dried ice cream has to be purchased. It can be found in some camping departments or stores, or from online resources, and I've even seen it in educational stores marketed as "Astronaut Food." The only freeze-dried ice cream I have personal experience with is Thrive, from Shelf Reliance. It has the consistency of the little marshmallows in Lucky Charms. The flavor, though, is exactly like that of ice cream. It has every day benefits, too. There are no dishes to wash up, it doesn't need to be prepared in any way - not even scooped. It is not messy, and it does not need to be frozen. How cool (no pun intended) to be able to give the kids an ice cream sandwich in a hot car on a summer road trip and not have it drip all over the car!

Freeze dried ice cream would make a lovely treat after working and living in the heat in a summer without power. (Photo Credit to Gustav H on Flickr)

If you are in the baking mood, consider baking up some of your family's favorite cookie recipes for the freezer. To avoid having one big cookie lump, freeze them individually first on a cookie sheet, then place them in a freezer container or bag. If you have the accessibility to cook them in a power outage and would rather enjoy them freshly baked, simply roll the dough into balls and freeze the same way – first on a cookie sheet, then stored in a freezer bag.

Turning Recipes into a Meal Plan

Earlier, in Chapter Four, we gave you several recipes that can be made in bulk and canned for storage, and here we have summarized the kinds of foods you can have on hand to keep meals relatively familiar, even in the worst of circumstances. This is all well and good, but if you don't have a plan for them, before you know it, you'll have nothing but a month of one kind of soup left on your hands. Let's look back at some of these recipes and see how they can fit into a week of meals, which can then be rotated into a full month.

DAY ONE: Pancakes/Ham and Beans. One decently sized ham –

$15-20 – and five pounds of dry beans will make a whole lot of soup. To mix it up a bit, add some stewed tomatoes (or juice or sauce) to the pot. To maximize your cost per serving, use more beans and less meat. This is a hearty return for little effort and cost and, like the other canned entrees, will be low-prep once it is time to eat. Pancakes, on the other hand, will need some preparation, so make sure you have a griddle on hand for your fire or other cooking source.

DAY TWO: Muffins/Chili. While you could make it under dire circumstances without a way to bake, it definitely expands your options if you can. Muffins are simple for starting your day, and they also make great take-along snacks for later on. Come dinnertime, the best chili is your own recipe, but make a huge batch when you are in the canning stage.

DAY THREE: Omelets/Beans and Wieners. Omelets are so hearty and really start a day well. Rounding off the day with this high protein dinner (and having leftovers for lunch the next day) will certainly keep you going.

DAY FOUR: Oatmeal/Taco Soup. Oatmeal provides a surprising amount of nutrients, stores well, and can be easily jazzed up with dehydrated fruits and honey for plenty of variation. Taco Soup also offers plenty of variety, so if you get creative with a few batches on preparation day, you will never be bored once it's time to eat.

DAY FIVE: Fruit and Bread/Beans and Rice. Dehydrated fruits are yummy, but consider keeping a garden growing and having seeds on hand. Fresh melons and berries for breakfast would be lovely, and if you have a way to bake, a fresh loaf of bread would top it off nicely. Beans and Rice make another easily stored, easily varied dish. As a bonus, together they form a complete protein for perfect nutrition.

DAY SIX: Scrambled Eggs/Vegetable Soup. Whether from egg powder or, if you are doubly prepared, fresh from your chickens, eggs are a quick and easy way to get a load of nutrition. Vegetable Soup is just as hearty, and though it takes a lot of work in preparation, it is so good and cans so well that, if you have the time, you should consider it anyway.

A note from Robin: I do this one with my garden fresh vegetables each summer, since they are going to be pressure canned anyway. If I use canned veggies, they will be twice canned, and that just seems mushy.

DAY SEVEN: Toast/Meatloaf. With some jams and jellies or maybe peanut butter and honey stored, toast can be an easy breakfast. Remember that you will not have access to a toaster, though, so try the griddle over the fire to warm up the bread. Extra bread may pair nicely with Meatloaf later on.

One big batch of each of these recipes should yield enough food to sustain your family for one month. Obviously, if your family is larger, make larger batches. One week of hard work and a bit of planning for cooking methods, and you will have a month's supply of meals on hand as well as a plan for using them. Simply rotate the week of meals into a month, with weekends sharing a "day." Remember to use those leftovers up so that you don't lose food to spoilage. This is a good practice even now – food is precious and should not be left to waste!

Breakfast Menu – One Month

S	M	T	W	Th	F	S
Pancakes	Muffins	Omelets	Oatmeal	Fruit & Bread	Eggs	Toast
Toast	Pancakes	Muffins	Omelets	Wheat Berries	Fruit & Bread	Eggs
Eggs	Toast	Pancakes	Muffins	Omelets	Oatmeal	Fruit & Bread
Fruit & Bread	Eggs	Toast	Pancakes	Muffins	Omelets	Wheat Berries

LUNCHES – Leftovers - Remember, no refrigeration!

Dinner Menu – One Month

S	M	T	W	Th	F	S
Ham & Beans	Chili	Beans & Wieners	Taco Soup	Beans & Rice	Veggie Soup	Meatloaf
Meatloaf	Ham & Beans	Chili	Calico Beans	Tacos	Beans & Rice	Veggie Soup
Veggie Soup	Meatloaf	Ham & Beans	Chili	Beans & Wieners	Taco Soup	Beans & Rice
Beans & Rice	Veggie Soup	Meatloaf	Ham & Beans	Chili	Calico Beans	Tacos

CHAPTER ELEVEN

FORAGING: EATING FROM THE YARD

Did you know nature has provided a grocery store in your own backyard? If absolutely necessary, a full and healthy vegetarian diet could be grown and sustained right from your garden, even if you don't have much space to work with. Educating yourself now on what can be foraged from existing plants and what you can grow to make things a bit easier will open up untold possibilities for you under dire circumstances. And even if the worst never happens, it can cut back on grocery bills now, as well as rounding out your diet to improve the health of your family. As much as we have talked about the importance of storage inside your home, the earth around you can be just as valuable.

Edible Weeds

I suspect that most of the weeds you mow, spray, and pull can actually sustain you in a major crisis at worst, or supplement your fresh produce at best!

Greenbriars have both curling tendrils and sharp thorns – an easy marker when
you are treasure hunting for dinner!
(Photo Credit to MichaelGras on Flickr)

A very common briar, commonly called Greenbriar, is something Brer Rabbit loved but we tend to hate. It is very persistent and very hard to kill — ask me how I know! But that can actually be a good thing. The leaves, stems and roots are all edible. The stems can be cooked like asparagus, the leaves like spinach, and the roots can used pounded and ground, using the gelatin as a thickener.

Another weed that is extremely common – look in your backyard — is Broadleaf Plantain. This is not the banana-like fruit you can purchase at the store. This is a free weed that has a multitude of food and medicinal uses. Cook the leaves like spinach, even going so far as to use it in recipes such as spinach dip or Creamed Spinach. Or, add the leaves to a tossed salad. Or, grind the seeds into flour. Or, cook the seeds like rice.

Other variations of Plantain "weeds" are also edible. Broadleaf is mentioned and pictured here, but also look for Ribwort (or Narrowleaf) Plantain, another common weed. (Photo Credit to calindarabus on Flickr)

Medicinally, plantain has so many uses that you really should cultivate it. Put it in a corner of your flower garden or vegetable garden and encourage it to grow! Used as a tea, it is an effective body detoxifier. As an ointment, it is a useful remedy for a long list of skin conditions. As a poultice, place directly on wounds.

Other edible weeds include dandelion, red clover, and stinging nettle. Plants like these are extremely hardy and surprisingly good for you. Try to identify edible weeds that thrive in your area to know what you can scavenge for (be careful in areas that may have sprayed pesticides or herbicides), and start now to cultivate some in your own yard.

Stinging Nettle is high in iron and makes a wonderful tea.
(Photo Credit to frankenstoen on Flickr)

Edible Landscaping

If you are already gardening, you have a great resource available right in your yard. But a victory garden doesn't have to come in traditional rows. You can turn your normal landscaping into an emergency food stash. Below are some notes adapted from Angela's book, **Backyard Farming in an Acre (Or Less)**, where she talks in depth about creating sustainability right on your property, even if it's not much space to work with. Adding edibles at your finger tips can be as simple as swapping out traditional landscaping type plants with edible alternatives.

GROUND COVER: Plant thyme or lettuce as a groundcover, creating a low maintenance source for herbs or meals.

FLOWERING PERENNIALS: Plant chamomile and Echinacea for both beautiful landscaping and beneficial medicinal herbs.

ORNAMENTAL ANNUALS: Swiss chard, basil, and cilantro are both attractive and delicious. So much flavor and nutrition never looked so good.

Gates, overhangs, walkways and fences all make lovely trellises for climbing fruits and vegetables. (Photo Credit to Keira on Flickr)

CLIMBING VINES: Climbing up the porch or arbor, try planting peas, pole beans, small squash, and grape vines.

LANDSCAPING SHRUBS: Elderberry, shrub roses, and blueberry plants are lovely shrubs that offer much more than looks.

ORNAMENTAL TREES: Small trees like crab apples and ornamental pears can be replaced with true fruiting counterparts such as peaches, pears, apples, and citrus. Dwarf forms can even be grown in large containers!

SHADE TREES: Traditional shade trees like catalpa, magnolia, and oak can be switched for nut-bearing alternatives such as pecan and walnut, or full-sized fruit trees.

When you are looking for ways to make the switch, think about what aspect of the ornamental plant you appreciate the most. Is it fragrance you enjoy? Try rosemary, old-fashioned roses, or elderberry. Is it colorful fruit that you appreciate? Consider persimmon, blackberries, or other edible fruits. Perhaps the foliage has a unique color like gray or purple? Plant lavender or tri-color sage.

Whatever your gardening or landscape situation, chances are there will be ways to include more edible plants into your traditional landscape design.

By using ninja-planting tactics, placing containers in otherwise unplantable situations, and being forward-thinking with your plans, your yard can provide you with added beauty and nutrients in even the bleakest of situations.

*— Adapted from **Backyard Farming on an Acre, More or Less** by Angela England. See the Resource section in the back of the book for purchase information.*

CHAPTER TWELVE
LAUNDRY IN EMERGENCIES

If the power is out for very long, even a few days, it becomes necessary to do some basic laundry. Maybe not the sheets and linens – they can hang out and "air wash." But the undies, a few pairs of jeans, some tee-shirts or sweatshirts…Some laundry cannot be ignored. There is no doubt that we can wear our clothes longer and more often between washings than we are used to. The first thing we'll learn about laundry when the power is out is to stall. But eventually, it will become inevitable. We have to wash something! Without electricity! Eeks!

Some people still have water even if the power is out, especially those living in towns with city water systems. But those of us that live out in the woods need electricity to run the water pump that allows water into the house. When we plan for a major power outage – one week or more – we have to consider how to do some laundry.

As part of your preparation plans, consider how you will do laundry without electricity. Do you live in a city? Will you have water?

Do you have a place to dry the laundry both inside and out (remember, it might be raining or freezing). What tools will be helpful?

- If you have a supply of microfiber towels on hand, you can use them in a power outage instead of regular towels, because the regular towels require more water to wash and have a longer drying time.
- Plan to wear your clothes longer.
- Wear layers, so that you will not have to wash the outside layer unless it gets dirt on it.
- Wear sanitary napkins to absorb moisture and odor, allowing you to wear underwear longer.
- "Air Wash" sheets and blankets, and anything else that does not have actual dirt on them. Air washing is simply hanging them outside to freshen them up.

Laundry Soap and Supplies

You will want to have some clean, five-gallon buckets, laundry soap (although we could survive a few weeks without it if we had to), and a plunger. A special laundry plunger would be best and can be purchased at Lehman's for less than $20, although a regular toilet plunger will work just fine.

A wringer of some kind will make rinsing the clothes much easier. You can spend $100+ for something fancy, or you can just have a mop bucket with a ringer or "squeezer" on it.

Homemade Laundry Soap

1 bar Fels Naptha or other type of soap
1 cup washing soda
½ cup borax powder
2-5 gallon buckets
A hand grater

Buckets of all kinds are extremely handy to have around. For laundry, a mop wringer is an added bonus. (Photo Credit to cogdogblog on Flickr)

Grate the bar soap into a small pot of water and heat until the soap is melted. Put the soap mixture into a 5-gallon bucket, add 1 cup washing soda and ½ cup borax to the solution. Add hot water and stir until powders are dissolved. Fill the bucket with warm water and stir thoroughly. Let sit overnight. The solution will become very gelatinous. The next day, pour half of the mixture into another 5-gallon bucket and fill both buckets up with warm water; stir. You now have 10 gallons of laundry soap.

A note from Robin: I stack the buckets on top of each other next to my washing machine. An alternative is to put the gelatinous solution into smaller containers –such as empty laundry soap bottle – and fill half with solution and half with water.

Use 1 cup of detergent per load. Do not expect bubbles – bubbles do not clean clothes anyway.

Tip: You can make homemade, "Oxyclean"-style stain remover with just a few items you probably already have on hand – one cup of water, plus a half cup of peroxide and a half cup of baking soda.

Washing Laundry Outside

- You will need to heat your water as much as possible to get it sanitized and truly clean.
- Add detergent to the water in one bucket, and leave another with only clean water.
- Place the article of clothing in the bucket of water.
- Agitate it in the buckets with detergent.
- Wring the water out before rinsing.
- Place the article of clothing in the rinse bucket, agitate, and wring out. Adding a cup of vinegar to the bucket of rinse water will help get the detergent out and will replace fabric softener.
- Hang the article up to dry in any way you can.

Drying Clothes Without Power

Regardless of the season or the weather, clothing can be dried on a line, either inside or out. Our first thought about drying clothes on a line is that of a nice, Spring day with the sun shining and breeze blowing. Springtime is a wonderful time of year for hanging out laundry. It's an especially fun and rewarding part of spring cleaning. There is nothing to match the sweet smell of freshly laundered linen after a winter of being closed up in the house! It isn't always Springtime when you need to dry your clothes outside, though, especially if your power outage is due to foul or freezing weather.

Drying inside takes a bit more ingenuity, and it's never very attractive, but line can be strung across any room. The room with a wood burning stove is ideal (and a wood-burning stove is an essential part of any long-term preparedness program!). It will add warmth and humidity to the room and make drying more efficient. Wooden racks can be purchased at the local variety store, and they can be folded and put away when not in use. In a pinch, you can lay the clothes out on quilting racks or repurposed step-stool ladders.

If you live in an area where outside line drying is prohibitive (and moving is not an option), at least have the materials and the know-how to build one if things change. Perhaps you could buy a portable camping clothesline. Surely, if the power is out for a week or more, your homeowner's association will cut you some slack!

Although a clothesline is not necessary, it certainly adds convenience and practicality. Materials to build a clothesline can be purchased at most variety or hardware stores. A good clothesline is strung between two well-anchored posts. A serviceable line is strung between anything available! If the line is strung taut, it will support the laundry by itself; if not, a post of some sort may be needed to prop up the line in the middle. Keep a rag on the line with a clothespin so that the line can be quickly wiped of pollen and dust before hanging out a new batch of laundry.

Make sure your line is high enough and tight enough so that even your biggest towels and linens do not drag the ground.

Another option for building a clothesline is to use a pulley system. With this method, you do not have to build or set poles. But while you don't have to invest in concrete, you do have to invest in the pulleys.

You can attach the pulley system to a tree outside your house and to a convenient door or window in the house. (Imagine clotheslines strung between two tall apartment buildings, so that you can pull the laundry in.) Or, you can attach the system between two trees.

My personal clothesline is the old-fashioned kind. It is made out of 4x4s set into the ground with concrete. They have an anchoring length of rope stretching from the post down to the ground at an angle. The only reason for this is to keep the poles from being pulled towards each other, which makes the lines sag from the weight of the laundry. Have you ever seen old pictures with sticks holding up the center of the clothesline because the lines are sagging so much that the clothes are touching the ground? If you don't want such a permanent structure, you can just put the poles in the ground without the concrete and use a forked stick to hold up the lines should they begin to sag.

A note from Robin: I like wooden clothespins. I don't have a reason — maybe it's just because they seem more "homesteadish." I like to have the clothespins easily accessible, which for this getting-old-and-hard-to-bend-body means having them hanging on the line as I am hanging out the linens.

A simple DIY pin-holder will make your clothesline much more convenient.

Clothespin bags can be purchased at the store. They have a hanger built-in so they conveniently hang on the line while you are hanging out the laundry. This prevents all of the bending over you would have if you kept the pins in a container on the ground.

A hanging clothespin container can easily be made out of empty bleach or other liquid detergent bottles. Cut a section out of the handle so that it will hang on the line. Cut another section out of the front of the bottle where the pins go, and you are done! To reduce the number of clothespins needed, overlap each garment and pin the two corners onto the line simultaneously, with one pin.

The length of time it takes to dry a batch of laundry obviously depends on the weather. A cool, dry day with a nice breeze is the best. An extremely hot day will dry clothes extremely quickly! When it comes down to it, though, in the absence of electricity, does it really matter how long it takes the laundry to dry on a line? It will eventually dry. Even if your electricity is up and running, line drying in nice weather will save on the electricity bill. According to the Consumer Energy Center,

> *"A dryer is typically the second-biggest electricity-using appliance after the refrigerator, costing about $85 to operate annually."*

Who couldn't find something more fun to spend that on?

CHAPTER THIRTEEN
BATTLING THE ELEMENTS

"Food, shelter, and clothing" is the cliché that first comes to mind when one ponders survival. We have covered food and clothing, along with many other things one might not have thought of when pondering one's own emergency preparedness needs. Yet, we have yet to discuss shelter, or in other words, surviving the elements. Preparing to endure the elements without electricity is really dependent on two variables: whether it is extremely hot or cold where you are, and whether your home is habitable.

Hot Weather Safety

Let's assume for the moment that your home is habitable. What can you do if it is extremely hot outside? Not much to cool off, but you can take steps to stay safe.
- Stay hydrated!
- Open windows and/or find a nice breeze under a shade tree
- Get up earlier to take advantage of cooler morning hours, and

learn rest during the heat of the day
- Learn about heat exhaustion, heat stroke, and the preventions and treatments for each

Hydration is extremely important in the heat, so be sure you have lots of water stored as summer approaches. As mentioned earlier, water can be canned or stored in empty bleach bottles. Other alternatives are purification tablets or purification straws. (Photo Credit to puroticorico on Flickr)

Heat Exhaustion

If you are working in the heat or if your home is too hot, you need to keep an eye out for heat exhaustion. It occurs when sweat cannot cool the body, and dehydration often follows. Some markers of heat exhaustion include profuse sweating, muscle cramps, weakness, lightheadedness, and headaches.

To prevent heat exhaustion, first drink plenty of water! Beyond that, try to do whatever needs to be done in the cool of the day, which is generally evenings, nights and early mornings. Rest a lot, and be sure you keep sweating, but be conscious of your body sweating too much.

Remember, we are discussing the possibility of medical attention not being available. So what can you do if you or a family member exhibit symptoms of heat exhaustion?

It is important to stop activity and move to the shade. To cool quickly, some clothing can be removed and the skin misted with water. Again, prevention is the best medicine, so exercise caution in extreme temperatures.

Heat Stroke

Heat stroke is a much more serious condition, but it can follow right on the heels of untreated heat exhaustion. Heat stroke is hyperthermia – the exact opposite of hypothermia. With heat stroke, the body's temperature gets too high and is unable to cool itself. Most people go through the signs and symptoms of heat exhaustion first, and then progress to heat stroke. That is why it is so important to recognize heat exhaustion so that appropriate treatment can be taken in order to avoid heat stroke. However, it can also onset suddenly, without any warning at all. Symptoms can vary, but according to the CDC, might include an extremely high body temperature; skin that is red, hot and dry, with no sweating; a rapid pulse and/or throbbing headache; dizziness, nausea, and confusion. Ultimately, it can progress to unconsciousness.

The primary prevention of heat stroke is to prevent heat exhaustion. Do not put yourself in the position to overwork and overheat your body. To repeat from above: prevent heat exhaustion by drinking water! Do whatever needs to be done in the cool of the day, rest a lot, and be sure you keep sweating, but at a normal – not excessive- pace.

So what to do if you recognize heat stroke in yourself or someone else? The CDC recommends the following steps:
- Get the victim to a shady area.

- Cool the victim rapidly using whatever methods you can. For example, immerse the victim in a tub of cool water; place the person in a cool shower; spray the victim with cool water from a garden hose; sponge the person with cool water; or if the humidity is low, wrap the victim in a cool, wet sheet and fan him or her vigorously.
- Monitor body temperature, and continue cooling efforts until the body temperature drops to 101-102°F.
- If emergency medical personnel are delayed, call the hospital emergency room for further instructions.
- Do not give the victim fluids to drink.
- Get medical assistance as soon as possible.

Sometimes, a victim's muscles will begin to twitch uncontrollably as a result of heat stroke. If this happens, keep the victim from injuring himself, but do not place any object in the mouth and do not give fluids. If there is vomiting, make sure the airway remains open by turning the victim on his or her side.

These conditions are not to be trifled with, so it is always a good idea to plan for a way to reach medical help if necessary. Find several routes to a hospital or clinic, make sure you have both a cell phone and access to a landline in case one is operable to call 9-1-1 or a physician, and include cooling supplies in your emergency first aid kit.

Cold Weather Safety

Let's continue to assume that your home is habitable, but now the weather is extremely cold. This is easier to endure than extreme heat, because it's easier to find ways to stay warm than to escape the heat. Hopefully you have prepared with either a wood heat source or a kerosene space heater *(with plenty of fuel! – See Chapter 7)*. You can also:

- Add more clothes
- Exercise (go chop some more wood!)

- Drink something warm
- Understand frostbite and hypothermia

A simple neckwarmer that can be pulled up to cover the face is extremely helpful. Fleece and felted wools will block the air better than loose knits.
(Photo Credit to lululemon athletic on Flickr)

Frostbite

Smaller, exposed portions of skin such as the nose, cheeks, chin, fingers, and toes, are susceptible to frostbite and should be carefully protected. This condition is the freezing of skin and tissues below the skin and can lead to infections and complications. Because symptoms include numbness, you often cannot tell you have it until someone points it out, so try not to be out in the elements alone. Symptoms begin with prickly, burning, or numbing sensations, and may include a red and splotchy appearance. From there, it progresses to include skin that may be grayish or yellow, firm and waxy, and ultimately completely numb.

"Frostnip," the less severe freezing that precedes frostbite, is more readily treatable by slowly pouring warm water on the affected area, so take symptoms seriously and treat affected skin before the situation escalates.

Frostbite can be coupled with hypothermia, so become familiar with all signs and symptoms. If there are no signs of hypothermia, the CDC recommends the following steps if medical care is not available:

- Get into a warm room as soon as possible.
- Unless absolutely necessary, do not walk on frostbitten feet or toes—this increases the damage.
- Immerse the affected area in warm—not hot—water (the temperature should be comfortable to the touch for unaffected parts of the body).
- Or, warm the affected area using body heat. For example, the heat of an armpit can be used to warm frostbitten fingers.
- Do not rub the frostbitten area with snow or massage it at all. This can cause more damage.
- Don't use a heating pad, heat lamp, or the heat of a stove, fireplace, or radiator for warming. Affected areas are numb and can be easily burned.

Hypothermia

If a person has been exposed to the cold long enough or for some reason has been submerged in cold water, hypothermia could follow. Defined as body temperature dropping from the average normal temperature of 98.6 degrees Fahrenheit to 95 degrees, hypothermia is very serious and should not be taken lightly. Much like frostbite, the affected person may not realize what is happening. Symptoms arrive gradually and progressively, so watch out for each other and avoid being alone in the elements.

Symptoms of hypothermia vary, but watch closely for any and all of them. Shivering is an early sign, along with clumsiness, slurred speech, stumbling, or confusion. Poor decision making can also be a signal of hypothermia, so strange behavior such as trying to remove warm clothes should be a concern. Low energy, apathy, a weak pulse, and slow or shallow breathing can all be indicators of advancing hypothermia, and a progression into unconsciousness is possible

If you notice any of these symptoms beginning in yourself or someone else, it is imperative to take immediate steps to regain warmth. It is much more likely that you will be able to bring a body temperature back up in the early stages than it will be once hypothermia has completely set in.

Treatment for hypothermia is "simply" to warm the person back up. Unfortunately, their body is in a delicate place, and you must handle them gently in order to prevent cardiac arrest. For example, wet clothing should be removed, but if it is too difficult to do so without shaking and jarring them, it should be cut off. Rubbing the skin or body is not helpful; instead, skin to skin contact with another person under a blanket will help to bring their body temperature back up. They should be covered with warm blankets and warm compresses (dry), kept off of the cold ground, and if they are alert they should be given warm, non-alcoholic and non-caffeinated beverages. As with any other major medical condition, make efforts to contact a physician or emergency services if you suspect hypothermia. Again, from the CDC:

"These procedures are not substitutes for proper medical care. Hypothermia is a medical emergency, and frostbite should be evaluated by a health care provider. It is a good idea to take a first aid and emergency resuscitation (CPR) course to prepare for cold-weather health problems. Knowing what to do is an important part of protecting your health and the health of others."

"Taking preventive action is your best defense against having to deal with extreme cold-weather conditions. By preparing your home and car in advance for winter emergencies, and by observing safety precautions during times of extremely cold weather, you can reduce the risk of weather-related health problems."

Shelter in Extreme Temperatures

What if your home is not habitable and the weather is extremely cold? The very best option is to have adequate home owner's insurance so you have the resources to relocate. If that is not possible, consider storing a high quality tent. Army tents, like the ones portrayed in the television program M.A.S.H., would be a great idea. Or, you can store materials to make a more primitive, temporary shelter. For a teepee shelter, you need tarps and poles that are long enough to make the teepee. Place the poles in the cone-like shape of a teepee, secure them, and wrap the frame with the tarps.

What if your stash has been destroyed with your home? Be prepared, both with knowledge and materials stored in a safe place, to build an outdoor shelter. With a bit of preparation, you can even have winter shelter in an urban environment, although living out in the country will make building an outdoor shelter easier.

A debris shelter is just like it sounds. You find a fallen tree that is safely leaning against a standing tree, and pile debris and brush in such a way as to make a shelter. If it is big enough, and you are using live vegetation, you can even have a small fire at the entrance for heat. Practice all year long, just in case – it could be fun for the kids to play in, or for a family campout in early fall.

Do not forget about heat. We've been assuming your home is habitable in extremely hot weather. If your home is not habitable, you need to keep trying to stay as cool as possible. Use a tent that you have previously obtained to stay shaded and dry in the rain, or be prepared to know how (and have the materials) to build a shelter. The rain may be a cooling relief, but you will need to protect your things and might not necessarily want to be soaked.

CHAPTER FOURTEEN
HEALTH AND SAFETY

Consider what the most likely emergency situations would be for your family. Does a family member have diabetes? High blood pressure? Weak joints? Severe depression? Gastric disorders? Is anyone pregnant? What if someone breaks a bone or receives a serious laceration? Are you prepared to handle a medical emergency at home, on your own?

Specific Health Conditions

While you can never guarantee perfect health, doctors and experts all agree that a good diet and physical exercise are vital components to a healthy lifestyle and can, in fact, deter and help to control many ailments. Preparing your home for the added supplies a power outage or disaster could bring will do little if you have not prepared your own body and health for the added work it would bring. From long-term health struggles to immediate injury or the temporary but vital needs to pregnancy, getting into shape now will make the adjustment feasible.

The number one best way to avoid medical disasters in the first place is to be healthy to begin.

Diabetes, High Blood Pressure, Heart Conditions

Many people manage conditions such as these primarily through diet and exercise. If you or someone in your household has such a condition, the best way to be prepared for a major emergency is to plan to maintain your current strategy. If your diet requires certain foods or meal frequency, make sure your food stores reflect that need. If you are currently on medication, be sure to have some stocked up, just in case.

Looking beyond thirty day preparation, if your concern is access to medication, it would be prudent to talk with your doctor about the possibility of weaning off of your medication through alternative means. If you cannot get off the medication, work with your doctors to at least try to lower the dosage and get you to a place where you could live without your medication for a couple of weeks in a drastic situation.

Physical exercise is a prominent contributor to overall health. Starting slowly with walking and then building up to more can improve your strength and health not only for emergencies but for life.
(Photo Credit to www.metaphoricalplatypus.com on Flickr)

Mental Health

These conditions are as real and serious as any of the others we have covered. You may be on prescription medication for mental health now, but consider what would happen if you did not have access to your medication for 2-4 weeks. Would you be able to cope? Would you become a danger to yourself or others? It is important to have an extra supply of medication on hand for an extreme situation. Beyond that, talk to your mental health provider about alternative ways to get you through a crisis.

As with other prescription medications, see if you can wean off by exploring alternative treatment with your doctor. If that is not possible, can your condition be managed in alternative ways, for at least for 2-4 weeks? A disaster situation will obviously add stress, so it is important that you consider all options and scenarios ahead of time.

Gastric and Internal Disorders

Stock your pantry with foods that are currently on your diet so that, in an emergency, you don't get sick. Store what you eat and eat what you store; you do not need a drastic change in diet during a disaster. Talk with your doctor about alternative treatments that do not require a prescription — treatments that can at least get you through 2-4 weeks without your medication.

Breaks, Sprains, Strains

Should you find yourself in a situation where you have to treat muscular/skeletal injuries on your own, do you have supplies? Look for splints, crutches, braces and pain management. But, again, the number one best way to avoid muscular/skeletal injuries is to be in good shape in the first place. In such a situation, you may be chopping wood or hauling water. If your muscles are not used to such workouts, you will be more prone to injury.

To be prepared, you do not need to do the latest "X-treme" workout or have a strenuous and time consuming regimen. A regular walking program is probably sufficient to ward off muscle strains in a disaster situation. Keep your joints loose, your muscles moving, and eat well to maintain healthy bone integrity. You will then be less likely to have a serious muscular/skeletal injury.

Pregnancy

Even if, and perhaps especially if, you favor hospital births, you need to be ready to deliver in an emergency situation without medical intervention, just in case. It is not at all unusual for a family to be snow-bound or ice-bound for several days. Could a baby come in your household during that time? Know your body, understand pregnancy and fetal development, and learn what is normal. Especially learn what is abnormal and what you can do about it. Work with your doctor or midwife to prevent or control gestational diabetes, toxemia and other complications of pregnancy. Have a plan ready just in case you find yourself unable to get medication or get to your doctor. Just in case.

Physical Skills to Learn and Practice

Plan ahead. Getting reasonably healthy and fit will go a long way toward preventing the need for extreme medical care in extreme emergency situations. Aside from storing meals that will fuel your health and medicine that will maintain it, having learned and practiced the more physical skills that you may need will help to prevent injury and shock. Regular exercise is always beneficial, but you will want to be familiar with the movements and exertion of some basic skills.

For example, if you find that you cannot carry a bucket of water, it is best to know now that you need a wagon or some apparatus to help you move it, rather than being blindsided in the moment. Chopping wood, pulling weeds, and carrying things back and forth can all be physically tasking if you are not used to exerting yourself. Build up stamina now with exercise and plenty of movement. The work will be difficult no matter what, but you will be glad you prepared your body if you start now.

CHAPTER FIFTEEN
MAJOR
FIRST AID

Imagine that there has just been major tornado, ice storm or earthquake near your home. The electrical power will be out for two weeks. During that two week period of time, you have run out of gasoline, the local gas station is also without power, and you cannot leave your home. Somebody in the family receives a major injury – a burn, a broken bone, or severe laceration. What are you going to do?

Basic First Aid Kits

Most of us have a home first aid kit. Bandaids and antibiotic cream are good, but that alone is not really very helpful for something major, even during normal times. We may treat minor injuries at home, and if these small injuries are left untreated, usually nothing happens. Even if a minor wound were to become infected, it is a simple matter to take the injured to the doctor, so our first aid kits are simple – something like:

- Bandaids and antibiotic ointment for minor wounds and abrasions
- Elastic tape for binding a sprained ankle or wrist
- Suture strips for holding together a minor cut
- Tweezers
- Scissors, etc.

A good first aid kit is important under normal circumstances; it is vital in a disaster. Keep it well-stocked and in your shelter or in a safe place so that you have access to it even if there is structural damage to the property.
(Photo Credit to Marcin Wichary)

Herbal First Aid

In addition to a home first aid kit, an herbal "first aid" kit is good to have on hand for emergencies. The following natural remedies are always good to have at home. Homeopathic remedies should not be stored next to strong smells, so keep your homeopathic tablets separately from your essential oils.

Essential oils can be very effective in treating many bacterial, viral, and other infections without causing resistance. The natural variation in the chemical constituents in whole plants depending on climate, altitude, and other factors protects against this resistance, as do the many chemical constituents in whole oils as opposed to using one isolated "active" ingredient.

One study compared the effectiveness of essential oils to antibiotics — preliminary results showed cinnamon and oregano are comparable with penicillin and ampicillin in inhibitory activity against e. coli and staphaureus. Tea tree oil (TTO) has been widely used in Australia for 80 years and is active against many micro-organisms.

Some herbal preparations you might consider keeping on hand include:

ALOE VERA - Aloe vera gel is a soothing remedy for sunburns and other types of burns. Grow your own aloe plant (Aloe barbadensis) at home or keep a jar of aloe gel in your natural remedy cupboard.

ARNICA CREAM/OINTMENT AND HOMEOPATHIC ARNICA TABLETS - Arnica cream (Arnica montana) is used externally on sprains, strains, bruises and sore muscles. Homeopathic arnica tablets are used internally for relief in injuries and shock.

ARSENICUM ALBUM HOMEOPATHIC TABLETS - A homeopathic remedy for stomach upsets such as diarrhea and food poisoning.

ECHINACEA (ECHINACEA ANGUSTIFOLIA/PURPUREA) - Echinacea has traditionally been used to boost the immune system and to fight off colds. The easiest way to take Echinacea is in tincture form. The tincture (diluted in water, follow instructions in the bottle) can also be used to gargle a sore throat and to clean cuts and small wounds. Echinacea is sometimes combined with Goldenseal (Hydrastis canadensis), another traditional folk remedy for colds and other upper respiratory tract infections. (Goldenseal is not recommended for pregnant or breastfeeding women.)

EUCALYPTUS ESSENTIAL OIL - Eucalyptus oil (Eucalyptus

globulus/radiata) is a great home remedy for colds, coughs and sinus infections when used in a steam inhalation or in a bath. It is also a natural insect repellent – the lemon-scented Eucalyptus citriodora is especially good for homemade bug repellents.

GINGER, PEPPERMINT AND CHAMOMILE HERB TEAS - Ginger tea relieves nausea, including travel sickness and morning sickness. Ginger tea is also a great help for colds and sore throats. Peppermint tea relieves indigestion, flatulence and travel sickness. Chamomile tea helps with diarrhea and other stomach upsets.

LAVENDER ESSENTIAL OIL (LAVANDULA ANGUSTIFOLIA/ OFFICINALIS/VERA) - Rub a drop of lavender oil on the temples to relieve headaches or make a Lavender compress to relieve muscle aches, headaches and period pains. Lavender oil is also a good home remedy for insect bites: a drop of pure Lavender oil on a mosquito bite relieves the itching.

PROPOLIS LOZENGES - Propolis lozenges are a gentle natural remedy for sore and irritated throats.

RESCUE REMEDY - Dr. Bach's Rescue Remedy (Recovery Remedy) is a safe natural first aid treatment in a shock or in any stressful situation. It also comes in spray form or as pastilles.

TEA TREE ESSENTIAL OIL - Tea tree oil (Melaleuca alternifolia) is antibacterial and antiviral. It is a traditional home remedy for colds and other respiratory tract infections (use it in a steam inhalation or in a bath), and it can be used to clean cuts and wounds (dilute it to avoid irritation). You can also use a drop of pure tea tree oil on a wart or on a cold sore.

Major First Aid

In our pretend scenario, it is essential to prevent major infections by using something such a well-stocked first aid kit; we cannot simply stick a bandaid on it or ignore it as we might under normal circumstances. Blood poisoning can develop quickly, and without access to professional medical attention, the situation can become quite serious. The same can be said for broken bones, severe lacerations and other major wounds. In the event that a minor injury becomes serious, or a major injury occurs, it is very important to be prepared to handle major injuries at home.

INFECTION - Obtain a supply of antibiotics for your stash. Talk to your doctor about providing a supply of antibiotics and how and when to use them properly. Also, be sure that you have plenty of supplies to keep a wound clean.

BROKEN BONES - Craft sticks make good splints for broken fingers. Wooden rulers or yard sticks work well for larger appendages. For an adult leg, something like a section of 1x2 lumber might be useful. A rolled up newspaper or magazine can provide stability in the place of a wooden splint. Regardless of what you are splinting, you will also need a type of tape to fasten the splints onto the broken limb.

SEVERE CUTS - The biggest danger with a big cut is infection.

The wound must be thoroughly scrubbed and washed. Hydrogen peroxide, alcohol and saline solution (for contact lenses) are all good options to have in supply. It is essential to get it cleaned out, and that hurts! If you can obtain a supply of lidocaine or other numbing solution, it would be a huge help for the injured person.

Once the cut is thoroughly cleaned, it needs to be kept clean. Ideally, you would have some suture kits and would be able to stitch it up. If not, you could sew it up with sewing thread and a sterilized sewing needle. If that is not possible, you can use super glue, but a word of warning: stitches allow a bit of air to get in and a bit of space for infection to get out. Not so with super glue. If you use this option, watch it very carefully, and re-open if an infection starts to set. If all else fails, a wound can remain open if you can keep it clean and still. This would require a large supply of antibiotic ointment and gauze bandages. To hold the gauze and the wound securely in place, stock up on self-sticking ace bandages. If you have antibiotics available, this would probably be a good time to administer them.

Armageddon Medicine, by Dr. Cynthia J. Koelker, is a book that, while carrying a dramatic title, offers a wealth of information on preparing yourself for emergency medical contingencies. It is absolutely possible to compile your own kit from a variety of sources, as well.

The biggest obstacle you will face is the need for medication. In a scenario where the injury is major, prescription antibiotics may be required. If one is doing some suturing or has suffered a major bone break, pain will be a factor. Pre-existing conditions may need an advance-stock of medicine so that ailments like heart disease, diabetes can be controlled more readily. These medications would need to be obtained ahead of time, and that presents a challenge. Some people share information about how to work with your doctor to stock pile pain medications, antibiotics, and other prescription medications, but you'll want to pay attention to things like legalities, expiration dates and working with your physician to determine what's best for your specific situation.

As always, learn ways that you can approach a given circumstance without medication. Coping techniques and natural methods for pain relief are absolutely skills to obtain if you anticipate being distanced from medical care for any amount of time. For example, if you are not opposed to alcoholic beverages, at least for medicinal purposes, it would be a good idea to have a bottle or two on hand to be used as an antiseptic and a mild sedative.

Unexpected Home Births

One of the most dramatic and important life changes you can experience is the birth of a child. With a power outage or emergency situation thrown into the mix, it can be stressful and scary to say the least, and rightfully so. Still, we cannot ignore that, whether you are planning a home birth or expecting to go to the hospital, unforeseen circumstances could lead to an unexpected, unassisted home birth.

In old movies, husbands and bystanders to a birth are often sent on a mission to "get some towels and boil some water." To this day, I am not entirely sure what the boiling water is for other than to keep hands busy, but towels are a definite necessity. Birth is not without messes, and even laboring can be if your water has broken or is leaking. Have a stack of clean towels and blankets ready for when the baby is born, too, to dry him off and keep him warm.

The ACOG recommends preparedness plans for expecting mothers, and it includes having a few tools on hand for more than just messes. In His Hands Birth Supply has good, affordable kits and individual supplies at decent prices, and according to the ACOG's statement on the subject, an obstetrician should be able to provide you with an emergency kit as well.

Some of the items that are included:
- *Underpads, or "Chux" pads*. These are more familiarly used for puppy training. Use them during labor, under the birthing mom during pushing, under the mom after baby is born, under the toddler who is potty training…Towels could serve the same purpose, but it is easier to dispose of most of the mess since your attention will be wrapped up on other things!
- *Hydrogen Peroxide*. Whatever the chux doesn't catch, the peroxide will clean. It is also a great antiseptic for mom and baby.
- *Bulb syringe, baby hat*. When baby comes out, you want to suction her nose and mouth with the bulb syringe, then dry her off and get a hat and blanket on her to keep her warm. Mom might

also want a fresh blanket as it is somewhat common to shake and feel chilled after birth.

- *Neonatal thermometer.* A fever can indicate infection, so it is a good idea to take mom and baby's temperature regularly until you can get to a care provider.
- *Feminine hygiene products for after birth.* Cloth pads are useful for afterwards (See tutorials in Chapter 8), but no matter what, you need to stock up on your pads of choice. Remember that tampons and cups are not an option after birth. Cloth diapers, especially prefolds and flats, are useful, as well.

There are other items not provided in a kit than can be helpful to have on hand.

- *Gloves.* Since you don't know exactly what the circumstances will be, it is a good idea to have some rubber gloves on hand for touching any exposed areas and the baby. Be sure to get latex free in case mom or baby (or anyone else!) have an allergy.
- *Bendy straws.* It sounds silly, but mom really needs to stay hydrated during birth, and drinking through a straw will get a lot more fluid in her than she would consume otherwise.
- *Food and liquid for mom.* Have snacks and hydration available for the laboring mom, and a meal with some orange juice for soon after the birth. She will need to recoup all of that spent energy. Again, it is also a good idea to have a thermometer on hand to watch for signs of infection during and after birth.
- *A flashlight and batteries.* If the power is out, you will want to see what is going on with mom and baby.

If you are unsure of what to get or how to prepare, talk with your care provider. Consider also talking with a midwife, even if you are not using one. Midwives are familiar with home births and may be able to give you their perspective.

Preparing Yourselves for an Emergency Birth

The best way to be prepared for an emergency birth is to prepare for birth itself.

If you are anticipating a medicated birth, you might want to prepare yourself for the instance where you have no access to epidurals or pain relievers. How might you like to cope? If you are planning a home water birth, plan an alternative in the instance that water is not available in those quantities. For example, towels soaked in hot water laid on your back or belly are a good choice for both pain relief and lessening your planned use of water.

It is also helpful to know the signs of a normally progressing labor so that you can gauge where you might be in the process. For instance, a classic sign of transition, the adjustment period taking the mom from active labor to the final stage, is the mother insisting that she "can't do it."

Birthing classes are always helpful, as well as books like Ina May's Guide to Childbirth and stories of unassisted births.

Especially if you have an expected high risk birth, please also take extra precautions and make plans to get to your care provider – such as keeping your vehicle full of gas, planning alternate routes, and considering evacuating your home and staying in a location close to your care provider if necessary.

CHAPTER SIXTEEN
NATURAL
DISASTERS

Some natural disasters are easier to prepare for these days than in the past. Back in the day, all we had to go on was the way the clouds looked. Now, we have emergency warning systems that are capable of notifying us of a serious storm, or the threat of one, in advance. However, once the storm hits, if the power goes out, you cannot watch the tracking on television or listen to it on the radio (unless you have a battery powered weather radio, that is). So, even with advanced warning, what can be done to prepare for a natural disaster?

Establish Your Safe Place

OK Storm Shelters outlines the criteria for a good safe room for severe thunderstorms and tornadoes:

> *"The safest spot in person's home is typically in the basement or storm cellar. For individuals that don't have a basement, the most interior bathroom is a good place to go. An inner hallway,*

closet or inner room which doesn't contain windows, are decent alternatives. The center of the room is the safest part of a room. Individuals should do their best to stay away from corners and windows. When they are able to, they should hide under furniture that is sturdy."

What if you do not have a suitable location within your home? Where will you go when the sirens sound? If you have the resources, having a storm shelter installed in your yard is a great way to go. If not, then perhaps your safe spot is the nearest public storm shelter in a community building or a school. It is *very important* that you know where it is and how you will get there.

What You Need in Your Safe Place

Consider the immediate needs of your family, which clearly is safety during the storm. You may need some blankets or pillows in your safe room to protect you from shattering glass, or even just for comfort. Children, especially, will benefit from their special comfort item. If possible, keep these items in your safe place. Have a favorite book, perhaps a rather long chapter book that your family enjoys, as a read-aloud. Perhaps some crayons and a coloring book is soothing for your child. It helps if the storm toy is different than their usual toys. This makes it special, which will give it more staying power. Electronic devices with a game that is reserved for special occasions might help your children be distracted from the stress of a bad storm. A snack might be a good idea, and keep your 72-hour bags ready in case you need to move from your safe place to a shelter.

Safe Place Supplies to Consider:
- *Food* – MREs, Freeze-dried food, anything that does not require water or heat to eat.
- *Water* – must be drinkable
- *Blankets*
- *Light source* – and batteries if needed.

- **Tools** – can opener, batteries, etc.
- **Baby needs** – liquid formula, diapers, wipes
- **A read-aloud book** – can be very soothing and a positive distraction while weathering the storm.

It is not likely that you will spend a great deal of time in your safe spot, but have enough basic supplies in there for at least 72 hours. That will keep you alive and barely comfortable until other logistics get sorted out.

Immediate Needs After the Storm

Whether you go to a safe house or your safe place is at home, consider what you will need after the disaster. The power will likely be out, so keep flashlights with working batteries in your safe room or with your emergency packs. Have the phone numbers of your insurance adjuster and utilities available as well. Perhaps they could be taped to the inside of a bathroom cabinet or a safe part of the house. Certainly, a notebook with important information should be included in a portable emergency kit.

Try to have a telephone that doesn't require electricity to operate so that you will be able to make the necessary phone calls right away, assuming the phone lines are functional. If you are able to remain at home, but the electricity is out, you will need some food and water as well. It generally takes 72 hours before assistance is able to get to most affected areas.

You can quickly assemble three days worth of separate components, such as freeze-dried food, water, and toiletries. Determine how much you will need for each member of your household. You will also want some light and a way to potty as pleasantly as possible.

A Reminder About Insurance

Please carefully go over your homeowner's insurance policy with your agent to know what you have. Do not rely on your understanding of the policy itself; get the agent to go over it with you detail by detail. As always, prepare for the worst. Our insurance includes emergency cash to get us to a hotel ASAP with food and clothing. (In the event of a major natural disaster, that ASAP might be longer than is convenient – hence the 3-day kits.)

Downed trees can wreak immense havoc, doing damage to homes and power-lines and blocking infrastructure for days at a time.

A note from Robin: *Our homeowner's insurance will pay our hotel bill until we find a rental, and then pay the rent up to a year. We will still be paying our mortgage payment, but we will not have to make double payments. We have full-coverage replacement value on our house, as well as the contents of the house. Know what you have so that you can know what to expect. If you are in a possibly flood-prone zone, strongly consider coverage in case of water damage.*

Natural disasters are frightening. They are unpredictable and powerful. They are dangerous. The only thing we can do is to prepare ourselves for the worst. By being prepared, we can keep our family as safe as possible and a little more at ease than we would be otherwise.

Pets and Emergency Situations

Do you have a plan in place to care for your pet in the event of a natural disaster? What if your home were to be destroyed in a fire or flood?

We may not have control over when a natural disaster strikes, but having an emergency plan in place can help you to successfully save all of your family members, including your pets. Establish your plan now, before the disaster occurs.

Have an Emergency Kit Prepared and Ready

An emergency kit for your pet should contain:
- Enough food and water for your pet to last at least several days
- A leash and collar or harness and/or a pet carrier
- Food dish and water bowl
- Your pet's current medical records
- Any necessary medications, enough to last at least 1-2 weeks
- A recent photo of your pet (to be used for identification in case your pet becomes lost)
- A basic first aid kit

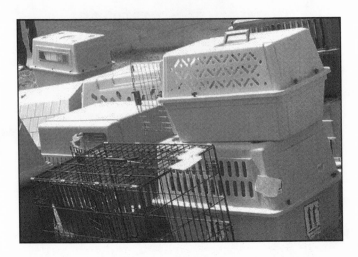

Pets are often displaced in major emergencies. Having a plan in place offers a better chance that your whole family stays together, pets included.
(Photo Credit to I See Things Differently on Flickr)

Plan for Housing

In the event of a mandatory evacuation, be sure you have a place to take your dog or cat. Check with local veterinary hospitals and kennel facilities for availability of boarding facilities. Contact friends or family members and ask to make arrangements to house your pet for a few days in the case of an emergency.

Be prepared to transport your pet to the prearranged housing facility. Do not rely on emergency personnel to take your dog or cat. They may have their hands full with human victims. Keep in mind that if the disaster is widespread, veterinary and kennel facilities near you may be affected also and may not be able to care for your dog or cat.

Do not count on being able to house your pet with your human family members if you need to take refuge in a shelter. Many of these shelters do not allow pets. In some cases, make-shift pet shelters may be provided to provide housing for displaced animals. If you need to take advantage of one of these shelters, be prepared to provide temporary housing for your pet such as a pet carrier or crate. Be prepared to show proper identification to enter the facility, and plan on visiting regularly to care for your pet.

Never Evacuate Your Home Without Your Pet

Even if you believe you will only be away from your home for a short period of time, never leave your pet behind. Always take your dog or cat with you if you need to evacuate. Emergencies can be unpredictable and if you are kept away from your home longer than expected, you will likely not be given the opportunity to return for your pet.

Make Sure All Family Members Are Aware of Your Disaster Plan

All family members should know your emergency plan, what needs to be done in case of disaster, and where to go during and/or after the emergency. A pre-arranged meeting place should be established in case some family members are separated.

CHAPTER SEVENTEEN
LEARNING TOGETHER ABOUT SURVIVAL SITUATIONS

Every journey has stops along the way, and a good journey is made great with people alongside you for the ride. While you could reasonably prepare for disaster, your level of efficiency under those circumstances would be hampered significantly if you had to catch everyone around you up as you went. Consider the morale difference for your family if everyone is familiar with the tasks and changes that would come into play, rather than being thrown into the unknown without any foundation of preparedness to build from.

Stopping with your family alone would be another mistake. Your community will feel closer than ever should grids and infrastructure go down. Why wait to learn with and from each other? The reality is that no single person has everything together. We all have different strengths and weaknesses. When put together, in our homes and communities, we fit like puzzle pieces, covering the gaps and strengthening our overall abilities.

Fun Family Preparedness Activities

Though a survival situation might be drastically different from your normal life, even if it is only for a week or a month, it does not have to be a shock. Making preparation fun now will make the changes familiar and even enjoyable should the time come to employ your new skills as a family.

Learn to cook over an open fire. Make this the plan for the next several Family Nights. You can involve the children in the prep, cooking and clean up. Be sure to do the entire meal with no electricity! You can even incorporate fire safety into the activity. To boost the preparedness level and build community, invite another family or two. Sing camp songs, tell stories, read aloud, and enjoy the time together.

Some meal ideas –

- Hot dogs, of course, but don't stop there. Make a lesson and game out of looking for appropriate sticks out in the woods. Have a whittling contest to get the ends pointy.
- Chili. Hang the pot over the fire to cook it. To involve your community, have a chili cook-off where families bring their favorite recipe.
- Stone soup. Again, hang a pot over the fire to cook, and invite other families to each bring a surprise ingredient (tell them ahead of time it's for soup or you might get candy or peaches). Put them all in the pot and cook – surprise! Also, you pretty much have to read Stone Soup aloud.
- Have a Dutch-oven dessert night. Prepare several coal beds, invite friends to bring their own dessert in their Dutch oven, and cook them all together. Tell stories or sing songs while you wait. Maybe you could even have a hayride!

Make a solar oven and bake a treat. Solar ovens can be made out of anything from a pizza box to plywood. Do some research on types of solar ovens and either build one or divide up and build a couple to see which model is best. It can take twice as long to bake in a solar oven as in a conventional oven, so make sure you allot enough time for building and baking on this productive and rewarding day.

Along with the food theme, sit down as a family to make your month's worth of menus, letting everyone choose their favorite. Include the children in making an ingredient list and going shopping. Here is the key to it: make it a fun trip. No one wants to go on a stressful, huge grocery shopping trip. Lighten the mood and enjoy yourselves! Set aside a special, visible place in your pantry that everyone knows not to dig into; that is your "Special Food."

As a bonus, make sure everyone picks a special meal or dessert that they are particularly looking forward to. It will be fun to rotate them into your regular meal plan for special days, and then you can have more fun family time picking another special dish to replace it in the pantry. In fact, it is a good idea to rotate your pantry stores into your meal plan anyway so that the foods are familiar. Be sure to only store foods that your family eats, and this will be even easier.

Go power-free. Turn off the main electrical switch on Friday night and don't turn it back on until Sunday night. While the power is out, make a list of all the things you wish had thought of for a power outage before. Spend the next few family nights shopping, planning and preparing, and then do it again. Did you fare better the second time than the first?

There are a few things that you can always build on to make a power outage better, and each of them can be fun to work on together:

- Compile family-favorite, non-electronic games. Spend your Family Night hunting for and playing a new game. From a traditional standpoint, you can never go wrong with Monopoly, Sorry and Uno. Or what about a chess/checkers set? And you can always learn or make up new variants on old games. Don't forget to retain the instructions. For something different, the company "Cooperative Games" creates and sells board games without the element of competition. The players all have to work together to win the game. Teamwork is essential in a disaster scenario, and this might give you a foundation to make work into a cooperative game.

Have family game nights now so that you know which games you really enjoy
playing together. Don't forget to stash some paper for scorekeeping!
(Photo Credit to a adamant on Flickr)

- Build a family library. Library access is something we take for granted, but if the power is out where you are, your library may be out of power, too. What are the family's favorite books? What books can be read over and over without becoming boring? What are your favorite read aloud books? Do you have a good selection of books for each reading level in the family, for all interests in the family? I only buy books that I know I will refer to as needed, or that are good enough to read over and over. Go on a scavenger hunt for certain books in a used book store, then make blanket forts or a fire and try them out as read-alouds.
- Collect music. Music is a terrific morale booster, but it takes power to play iPods and CDs. Instead, collect any instrument that anyone in your household knows how to play, along with a collection of music. If you have the ability to put together a small band,

be sure you have appropriate copies of music for each member of the group. Sing-alongs are never corny if you've been without power for a week. If you are really confident, pick up an instrument at a yard sale, collect lesson books and other music, and just store them. If the power is out for a long time, you will have time to finally learn to play!

Build self-sufficiency together. If you are planning for more than 30-days, it only makes sense to start in on some of the more permanent sources of self-sufficiency. Build a chicken coop together and hatch eggs, with everyone waiting and anticipating those first peeps through the shell. Teach the children now how to care for livestock, whether your own or through trips to neighboring farms. Learn to fish by, well, going fishing, and build a worm bed (which will also benefit your garden) so that bait is always available. If any of these skills becomes essential, they will already be comfortable with their jobs.

Learn to be outside. Camp (yuck!), even if you don't already love it (yuck!!), or maybe especially if you don't love it (seriously: yuck!). While you are out there, go for a hike. This not only gets children familiar with the outdoors, it builds stamina and strength. Before you go, learn about edible weeds in the area, even if it is your own backyard. For lunch, go on a treasure hunt for them and bring the goods back for a big picnic salad.

Go on a yard sale or thrift shop scavenger hunt. Take your list of items to watch for, split it up so that each family member has a small list, and spend a Saturday morning scouring local yard sales and thrift shops for deals. A prize system could make it even more fun – the person with the most finds picks dessert for the night (bonus if it is from the pantry!), the person who found the best deal picks the family game, etc.

Make a family emergency plan. In the scenarios we are talking about, your regular family routine will be disrupted. Keeping track of everybody will be challenge outside of your routine. You need to develop yet another plan! Include test runs and fire safety. While you are at it, have fun with fire extinguishers as you learn to use them. Learn how to safety light candles and lanterns and carry them from room to room. Muscle memory is important; everyone is much more likely to retain something they have done than something they have read. When your plan is set, create a babysitter folder that you can leave out in a conspicuous place. That way, your family will be safe even if you are not home.

Different scenarios may warrant different plans, so make sure you keep the variants in mind as you build your plans and practice your knowledge.

Fires

- Make sure you have a fire evacuation plan. Be certain, absolutely certain that every person in the household knows how to get out of the house. Teach them out to unlock and open windows and doors. Teach them how to safely break windows if necessary, by wrapping their arms or legs in a shirt, jacket or towel. In reality, it is better for them to get cut than to not get out.
- Select a meeting spot away from the house. This is extremely important so that you can count heads. You do not want to send a fireman into a burning house unnecessarily, so be certain everyone is accounted for.
- Never go back into the house for anyone, anything, or even pets. This is a hard concept for us as adults to grasp, and even harder to teach a child to not go back for Kitty. But it is imperative you wait for the professionals. They have a much better chance of getting your missing person out safely; if you go in for them, the chances are greater that you will both perish.

- Have fire drills. Yes, at home! Start with planned ones and then graduate to unplanned ones.

A note from Robin - A funny and slightly disturbing anecdote: My family often participated in national homeschool basketball tournaments. At one such tournament, the college arena, seating several thousand, was filled to capacity. The fire alarm went off. Thousands of homeschoolers sat around and looked at each other -- since they had never been to public schools, they had never had fire drills! We had to be told to evacuate. Fortunately, it was a false alarm and all was well. Don't let this be your family!

- Have fire extinguishers and teach everyone how to use them. Do NOT keep them above or near your oven! Should a fire break out there, you would not be able to reach them. Have the type of fire extinguishers that work for all types of fires, and then you won't have to worry about which type to use on which fires.
- Have burn ointment on hand – or some aloe plants – to treat small burns from small fires.

Tornadoes

- Know where to go. The lower the better, so if you have a basement or crawl space, that's where you should go. If not, do you have a room in your house that is inside, with no external walls and/ or windows? Look at your bathrooms. That's probably where you should go. If you go to a community shelter, do you know where it is? Could the children find their own way there if you were not at home?
- Have family tornado drills. Just like fire drills, start out with planned drills and then progress to surprises.
- Teach everyone to quickly grab a pillow and blanket. Better yet, have some in your safe place already. The pillows and blankets serve two purposes. First, you can cover yourself to protect from

breaking glass or flying debris. Second, they will help keep the chill off after the storm.

- Create your grab-n-go bags and teach the children where they are.
- Show the children the way to the community storm center, in case they have to go there alone or with a babysitter.
- Teach the family how to understand the weather reports on television, internet and radio. Show them on maps where you live and teach them how to spot your county.
- Learn how to watch for a storm in case the television is out. Even if the weatherman is not paying attention, or if you do not have access to him, it is no excuse for not realizing that it is storming and you should go to your safe spot. Having a battery-powered *(stock up on batteries!)* weather radio will help to solve this problem, as well.
- Understand how the tornado sirens work in your community. Learn what they sound like. Ask the emergency responders in your area if there are different sounds for different emergencies, and learn the difference. Some communities test the sirens on a specified day and time each week. Know the difference between tests and the real thing.

Power Outages

- Teach the children to freeze if the power goes out. Have games (drills in disguise) where they freeze where they are until you touch them. Take a bit longer to find them each time so that they will not panic during the real situation if you are not there immediately.
- Letting each child have their own flashlight is a good idea in theory, but getting them to leave them alone for emergencies is a challenge. Consider keeping them with batteries, etc, in a special place, where they only can come out during random flashlight playtimes after dark, with a code name letting them know it's flashlight time. Have them find things using the flashlight so that they learn to

use them purposefully and not just haphazardly. When the power goes out, use your code word and it will be a familiar game to them. Candles, lanterns, oils, wicks, and matches should also have a special place that everyone knows how to access.

- Have or make candles in containers that are suitable for a child to handle, light and carry around. A votive candle in a half-pint canning jar is perfect for small hands.
- As soon as you feel your child is old enough, teach them to strike a match and light a candle. Teach them to keep their hair and the cuffs of their sleeves away from the flame.

Don't underestimate the abilities of your child. Pioneer children were cooking over open flames with long skirts! Laura Ingalls Wilder was doing so at age 6. Don't think that your six-year-old is too young to be prepared.

Learn and Grow With Your Community

Working together as a family toward a common goal can build lasting bonds and memories that little else can. If you are well prepared as a family, you are in a position to help those around you. Particularly if you live in an urban area, it is almost as important that you know how to work with the community as your own family. No matter where you live, learning what resources your community has and what it needs is the last part of your preparedness plan - but no less important.

See what resources your community has in place already. Start by calling City Hall or the County courthouse. If you start asking questions about a preparedness plan, it is likely that the first couple of people you talk to won't have any idea what you are talking about. Just keep trying. Use phrases like "emergency preparedness plan," "emergency services," or "crisis management." Find out if your community has a search and rescue team. If so, how can you help? If not, how can you initiate one?

Become familiar with emergency services. Make friends with your local fire department, and learn what they would have you do in a given situation. Ask about ambulance services. Plan a group field trip to the local dispatcher. Let the children pretend to call, and get the advice of the dispatcher as to how you should best train them. Ask them whether, in your particular situation, it will be best to wait for the ambulance to get to you in an emergency or if you should meet them somewhere. Find out if your 911 service automatically brings up the street address; if not, you need to teach the children to repeat their individual addresses.

A community garden can provide a wealth of resources, not only in food but in learning opportunities for families and children. As you can see, a raised bed garden can be started nearly anywhere.
(Photo Credit to Daquella Marena on Flickr)

Find ways to enrich or establish community resources. Once you know where the community safe place is, see if there is a place to store any provisions. Work with neighbors and friends to gather donations to keep in the safe place. If space is not available, offer to teach classes to the community on how to prepare a grab and go bag. Consider a community garden to boost provisions and have the garden as a living resource in time of need. Take advantage of existing Boy Scout and Girl Scout troops, 4-H organizations, and other such organizations in your community. This will give children basic survival skills and rural living skills that will benefit them for years to come.

Seek out educational opportunities. Find out if your community has a Crisis Emergency Services. These organizations are trained to manage large crisis, such as a train/plane wreck, a terrorist attack, or the aftermath of a major storm. They often offer classes in first aid, evacuation plans, and general management issues. Learn what you can, and then offer to teach others.

And that is really the crux of all of this: learn what you can, and offer to teach others. No man lives on an island, yet so often we act as if we do. Life has become automated, and we seem to have lost our desire to live and work together. Take away electricity, basic infrastructure, and all such familiar services, and we are left only with each other. As you prepare your home and life for the unpredictable, remember that bonds with family and community are vital. Learn with each other; learn from each other; learn to lean on each other. With that, you might find yourself prepared for much more than 30 days of a physical storm.

GETTING PREPARED
APPENDIX

APPENDIX A
ESSENTIAL ITEMS FOR EMERGENCY SITUATIONS

ESSENTIAL ITEMS FOR
EMERGENCY SITUATIONS

Kitchen

o	Utensils (can openers, mixers)	o	Canning supplies (including jars/lids/wax)
o	Cast iron cookware	o	Fueled cookstove(s)
o	Aluminum foil	o	Paper goods
o	Canned foods	o	Sweeteners
o	Beans	o	Grains
o	Nuts, nutbutter	o	Tuna fish in oil
o	Snacks (jerky, trail mix, crackers, popcorn)	o	Milk – powdered & condensed
o	Vegetable oil	o	Spices and baking supplies
o	Graham crackers, saltines, pretzels, trail mix/jerky	o	Wine/liquors (for bribes, medicinal, etc,)
o	Breadmaking supplies (flour, yeast, salt)	o	Soup-base (bouillon, gravy)
o	Soy sauce, vinegar	o	Water enhancers (tea, tang, punch, cocoa)
o	Coffee	o	Wine, liquors (medicinal, trading)
o	Chewing gum, candies		

Clothing/Personal

o	Baby supplies: diapers/formula/ointments/aspirin, etc.	o	Heavy duty work clothes
o	Work boots	o	Thermal underwear
o	Woolen clothing and warm accessories	o	Gloves for work and warmth
o	Hats & cotton neckerchiefs	o	Rain gear
o	Socks, underwear, t-shirts, etc.	o	Mosquito coils, repellent, sprays, creams
o	Toilet paper, Kleenex, paper towels	o	Feminine hygiene products
o	Baby wipes, oils	o	Waterless & antibacterial soap
o	Hair, skin, and dental care products	o	Backpacks, Duffel Bags
o	Shaving supplies	o	Reading glasses
o	Atomizers for cooling/bathing		

Household Items

o	Generators	o	Propane cylinders & handle holders
o	Lantern mantles	o	Gasoline containers (plastic & metal)
o	Fire extinguishers (or a large box of Baking Soda in every room)	o	Carbon Monoxide alarm
o	Roll-on window insulation kit	o	Coleman's pump repair kit
o	Hand pumps & siphons (for water and for fuels)	o	Portable toilet(s)
o	Laundry system (washboard, bucket, plunger, wringer)	o	Clothespins/line/hangers
o	Bleach (plain, NOT scented: 4 to 6% sodium hypochlorite)	o	Laundry detergent (liquid)
o	Water containers	o	Water filters/purifiers
o	Garbage bags	o	Non-hybrid garden seeds
o	Garden tools & supplies	o	Batteries
o	Insulated ice chests	o	Garbage cans - plastic
o	Duct tape	o	Scissors, fabric & sewing supplies
o	Tarps	o	Stakes, twine, nails, rope, spikes
o	Sleeping bags & blankets, pillows, mats	o	Cots & inflatable mattresses

Fuel and Tools

o	Seasoned firewood	o	Bow saws, axes and hatchets, wedges
o	Honing oil	o	Lamp oil, wicks, oil lamps
o	Charcoal, lighter fluid	o	Candles
o	Matches	o	Coleman fuel
o	Lantern hangers	o	Lumber of all types
o	Flashlights/lightsticks & torches	o	"No. 76 Dietz" Lanterns
o	Defense and hunting tools (guns, ammunition, pepper spray, knives, clubs, bats & slingshots)	o	Knives & sharpening tools (files, stones, steel)
o	Fishing supplies/tools	o	Rat poison, mousetraps
o	Ant traps & cockroach magnets	o	Screen patches, glue, nails, screws, nuts & bolts

Misc. Supplies

o	Survival guide book	o	Boy Scout handbook, leader's catalog
o	Writing paper and utensils	o	Journals & scrapbooks
o	Calculators	o	First aid kits
o	Vitamins	o	Big dogs (and plenty of dog food)

o	Board games, cards, dice	o	Meals Ready to Eat (MREs)
o	Cigarettes (for trading)	o	Bicycles and supplies
o	Wagons & utility carts	o	Chickens
o	Livestock		

Preparation Readiness Key:

100% - Surviving in Style (with spares to share!)

>75% - FEMA has nothing on you.

50-75% - Ahead of the outbreak, but wishing for Walmart

25-50% - Smelly and sleepy, but somehow surviving

<25% - The Zombies win.

APPENDIX B
YARD SALE CHECK LIST ORGANIZER

Yard Sale
CHECK LIST
ORGANIZER

Check List

- o   Clothes - plan for growth
- o   Blankets
- o   Sheets
- o   Tarps
- o   Ropes
- o   Bungee cords
- o   Kerosene lamps
- o   Old candles can be melted down for new candles or fire starters
- o   Small jars/votives suitable for remaking candles
- o   Bicycles - can be rigged up for energy generator if you are resourceful
- o   Canning jars and rings
- o   Tools that do not require electricity
- o   Board games
- o   Toys
- o   Books
- o   Sheet music/books
- o   Supplies to build animal pens
- o   Exercise equipment
- o   An old ironing board would make a good back-board for a serious injury

Extras

Anything else the from Emergency Supplies Checklist or First-Aid Checklist you do not yet have.
Make note of needed items to keep an eye for here:

APPENDIX C

ESSENTIAL ITEMS FOR A HOME FIRST AID KIT

Build A Home
FIRST AID KIT
ESSENTIAL ITEMS FOR YOUR OWN KIT

Build Your Kit

o   Elastic bandages

o   Cloth and triangle bandages

o   Medical tape

o   Betodine

o   Anti-itch cream/ointment

o   Antibiotic cream/ointment

o   Pain medication

o   Cold medication

o   Allergy medication

o   Prescription medication

o   Antibiotics

o   Aloe vera gel or plant or other burn ointment

o   Saline (contact lense aisle) for washing out cuts or eyes

o   Instant cold packs

o   Antiseptic wipes/alcohol prep pads

o   Thermometer

o   Gauze sponges

o   Gloves

o   Scissors

Long Term First-Aid Considerations

o   Finger splints or craft sticks

o   Magazines/larger boards for larger splints

o   Suture kit

o   First-aid manual

APPENDIX D
RESOURCES

General Survival and Prepping Resources

SURVIVAL SPOT - http://www.survival-spot.com/

SURVIVAL CENTER - http://www.survival-center.com/

THE SURVIVAL MOM - http://thesurvivalmom.com/

EQUIPPED TO SURVIVE - http://www.equipped.com/medical.htm

THE SURVIVAL BLOG - http://www.survivalblog.com/

AMERICAN PREPPER'S NETWORK - http://americanpreppersnetwork.com/

HILLBILLY HOUSEWIFE - http://www.hillbillyhousewife.com/

BACKYARD FARMING ON AN ACRE (MORE OR LESS) - http://amzn.to/147q9Pn

WILD WOOD SURVIVAL - http://www.wildwoodsurvival.com/

SELF RELIANCE BY JAMIE - http://selfreliancebyjamie.blogspot.com/

Feminine and Infant Hygiene

MENSTRUAL CUPS - http://menstrualcups.wordpress.com/

CLOTH MENSTRUAL PADS - http://www.comfyclothpads.com/

DIY CLOTH MENSTRUAL PADS - http://www.sleepingbaby.net/jan/Baby/PADS.html

CLOTH DIAPERING INFO AND PURCHASE - http://www.kellyscloset.com/

Medical Resources

CDC EMERGENCY - http://emergency.cdc.gov/

MAYO CLINIC - http://www.mayoclinic.com/

ARMAGEDDON MEDICINE - http://armageddonmedicine.net/

University Resources

UNIVERSITY OF OK, FIREWOOD BROCHURE - http://bit.ly/Wh-6PvP

MSU, CANNING BROCHURE - http://bit.ly/UmppSI

Purchasing

LEHMAN'S - https://www.lehmans.com/

HOMESTYLE MERCANTILE - http://www.homestylemercantile.com/

IN HIS HANDS BIRTH SUPPLY – http://inhishands.com/

CHURCH OF JESUS CHRIST OF LATTER DAY SAINTS - http://bit.ly/Kp9mzG

SHELF RELIANCE - http://www.shelfreliance.com

ALL AMERICAN CANNER - http://www.allamericancanner.com/

Cooking Resources

CHEF TESS, 52 METHOD - http://cheftessbakeresse.blogspot.com/p/52-method-recipe.html

DUTCH OVEN DUDE - http://dutchovendude.com